Apr 21

Family Separation and the U.S.–Mexico Border Crisis

Recent Titles in
21st-Century Turning Points

Family Separation and the U.S.–Mexico Border Crisis

Laurie Collier Hillstrom

21st-Century Turning Points

ABC-CLIO®

An Imprint of ABC-CLIO, LLC
Santa Barbara, California • Denver, Colorado

Library of Congress Cataloging-in-Publication Data

Names: Hillstrom, Laurie Collier, 1965- author.
Title: Family separation and the U.S.-Mexico border crisis / Laurie Collier
    Hillstrom.
Other titles: Family separation and the United States-Mexico border crisis
Description: Santa Barbara, California : ABC-CLIO, 2020. | Series:
    21st-century turning points | Includes bibliographical references and
    index. |
Identifiers: LCCN 2020006070 (print) | LCCN 2020006071 (ebook) | ISBN
    9781440876615 (hardcover) | ISBN 9781440876622 (ebook)
Subjects: LCSH: Immigrant families—Government policy—United States. |
    Refugee families—Government policy—United States. | Illegal alien
    children—Government policy—United States. | Refugee
    children—Government policy—United States. | Detention of
    persons—Government policy—United States. | Alien detention
    centers—Mexican-American Border Region. | Mexican-American Border
    Region—Emigration and immigration.
Classification: LCC JV6483 .H555 2020 (print) | LCC JV6483 (ebook) | DDC
    362.89/9105610973—dc23
LC record available at https://lccn.loc.gov/2020006070
LC ebook record available at https://lccn.loc.gov/2020006071

ISBN: 978-1-4408-7661-5 (print)
      978-1-4408-7662-2 (ebook)

24 23 22 21 20   1 2 3 4 5

This book is also available as an eBook.

ABC-CLIO
An Imprint of ABC-CLIO, LLC

ABC-CLIO, LLC
147 Castilian Drive
Santa Barbara, California 93117
www.abc-clio.com

This book is printed on acid-free paper ∞

Manufactured in the United States of America

Contents

Series Foreword

21st-Century Turning Points is a general reference series that has been crafted for use by high school and undergraduate students as well as members of the general public. The purpose of the series is to give readers a clear, authoritative, and unbiased understanding of major fast-breaking events, movements, people, and issues that are transforming American life, culture, and politics in this turbulent new century. Each volume constitutes a one-stop resource for learning about a single issue or event currently dominating America's news headlines and political discussions—issues or events that, in many cases, are also driving national debate about our country's leaders, institutions, values, and priorities.

Each volume in the *21st-Century Turning Points* series begins with an **Overview** of the event or issue that is the subject of the book. It then provides a suite of informative chronologically arranged narrative entries on specific **Landmarks** in the evolution of the event or issue in question. This section provides both vital historical context and insights into present-day news events to give readers a full and clear understanding of how current issues and controversies evolved.

The next section of the book is devoted to examining the **Impacts** of the event or issue in question on various aspects of American life, including political, economic, cultural, and interpersonal implications. It is followed by a chapter of biographical **Profiles** that summarize the life experiences and personal beliefs of prominent individuals associated with the event or issue in question.

Finally, each book concludes with a topically organized **Further Resources** list of important and informative resources—from influential books to fascinating websites—to which readers can turn for additional information, and a carefully compiled subject **Index**.

These complementary elements, found in every book in the series, work together to create an evenhanded, authoritative, and user-friendly tool for gaining a deeper and more accurate understanding of the fast-changing nation in which we live—and the issues and moments that define us as we move deeper into the twenty-first century.

CHAPTER ONE

Overview of Family Separation and the U.S.–Mexico Border Crisis

Immigration occupies a unique space in U.S. history and American heritage. As a country founded and built by immigrants, the United States cultivated a reputation as a land of freedom and equality, a melting pot of diverse cultures and traditions, and a place that afforded hardworking individuals the opportunity to succeed and prosper. The Statue of Liberty embodied these ideals and stood as a beacon of hope to generations of newcomers from around the world. "My fellow Americans, we are and always will be a nation of immigrants," President Barack Obama declared in a 2014 speech. "We were strangers once, too. And whether our forbearers were strangers who crossed the Atlantic, or the Pacific, or the Rio Grande, we are here only because this country welcomed them in and taught them that to be an American is about something more than what we look like, or what our last names are, or how we worship. What makes us Americans is our shared commitment to an ideal, that all of us are created equal, and all of us have the chance to make of our lives what we will" (Obama 2014).

The United States remained a premier destination for immigration into the late twentieth and early twenty-first centuries, as millions of people came from all over the world in pursuit of the American dream. As immigration rates soared, however, an increasing number of U.S. citizens and political leaders expressed concerns about the impact these newcomers had on American society. Some critics claimed that immigrants took jobs from deserving Americans and burdened public health, education, and social services. Others complained that immigrants failed to assimilate, clung to their original languages and traditions, and eroded the nation's cultural unity. Such concerns generated growing support for efforts to restrict immigration to the United States. "America has changed dramatically . . . in ways that make us a mature society and render our past experience with immigration irrelevant," said Mark Krikorian of the Center for Immigration Studies. "We have outgrown mass immigration. It was an important phase of our national development, and played an important part in shaping who we are as a nation. But, like other phases we've passed through as a people—pioneers, settling the frontier, for instance—it's something we need to put behind us" (Krikorian 2008).

The opposing perspectives in the decades-long national debate over immigration came into sharp relief during the presidency of Donald Trump. The Republican businessman and television personality made immigration the centerpiece of his successful 2016 election campaign. In speeches, rallies, and social media posts, Trump consistently framed both legal and illegal immigration as threats to national security, public safety, and the U.S. economy. Trump vowed to build a wall to secure the 1,900-mile U.S.–Mexico border, which he portrayed as under assault by dangerous criminals, violent gangs, drug cartels, and terrorists. He also promised to step up efforts by U.S. Immigration and Customs Enforcement (ICE) agents to identify, locate, arrest, and deport the estimated 11 million people living in the United States without legal status. Immediately after taking office, Trump enacted a "travel ban" that temporarily halted immigration and restricted travel to the United States by citizens of seven predominantly Muslim nations. The Trump administration also placed new restrictions on asylum applications and drastically reduced the annual cap on the number of refugees admitted into the United States.

Supporters argued that these measures reversed decades of weakness, indecision, and political paralysis that prevented meaningful reform of the nation's outdated immigration system and allowed undesirable immigrants to overrun the country. Critics of Trump's immigration policies, on the other hand, asserted that his words and actions stoked fear and bigotry among his followers, fed nativist sentiments, and elevated anti-immigrant views into the mainstream. They claimed that Trump vilified and dehumanized foreign-born people and their descendants, fueling racial and ethnic tensions and creating a hostile environment for immigrants in the United States. "Through demagoguery and sheer force of messaging, Trump has upended many decades of bipartisan consensus in favor of immigrants and immigration, swinging the pendulum on an issue that is fundamental to America's vision of itself," Julie Hirschfeld Davis and Michael D. Shear wrote in *Border Wars*. "Since the country's founding, immigration has been at the heart of the American ideals of freedom and democracy, diversity and inclusion, opportunity and upward mobility. But it has also been at the core of the nation's struggles with its own identity, at times yielding darker moments in which leaders have turned inward in hopes of preserving a bygone era. Trump is one of them" (Davis and Shear 2019).

Family Separation and Child Detention

Of the many changes to U.S. immigration policy initiated by the Trump administration, the "zero tolerance policy" enacted in May 2018 stands among the most controversial. This policy required U.S. Customs and Border Protection (CBP) officials to arrest, detain, and prosecute anyone caught crossing the border without authorization. Enforcement of this policy proved complicated, however, because federal laws and court rulings established special protections for migrant children who entered the country illegally, whether unaccompanied or as part of family units. The Flores Settlement Agreement (FSA), for instance, limited the amount of time minors could be kept in immigration detention facilities to 20 days. To comply with the FSA, previous administrations generally released all family members from immigration custody within 20 days and allowed them to remain in the United States while awaiting their asylum or removal hearings—a process that could take years. Detractors referred to this policy as "catch and release" and claimed that it created a powerful incentive that drew record numbers of migrant families and unaccompanied minors to the United States. Trump administration officials blamed the catch-and-release loophole for overwhelming immigration enforcement resources and causing a humanitarian crisis at the border.

Due to its conflict with the FSA and other legal standards for the treatment of migrant children, the zero tolerance policy effectively forced immigration officials to separate migrant families that entered the United States together. When adult family members were arrested and prosecuted for the misdemeanor crime of illegal entry, their children became unaccompanied minors subject to the FSA restrictions on child detention. The parents remained in federal custody to await immigration hearings, while the children were released and sent to shelters operated by the Office of Refugee Resettlement. The zero tolerance policy thus became known as the family separation policy, as it resulted in more than 2,000 migrant children being taken away from their adult caregivers over the six-week period between May 7 and June 20, 2018. Administration officials argued that they were only enforcing U.S. immigration laws as written. They demanded that Congress pass legislation to allow families to be detained together or approve funding to expedite the processing of asylum requests. Some administration officials blamed adult migrants for family separation, arguing that they knowingly put their children in harm's way by crossing the U.S. border. Others claimed that smugglers, gangs, and cartels exploited legal protections for child migrants to gain entry to the United States.

As its effects became clear, however, the Trump administration's zero tolerance policy came under intense criticism. Opponents characterized the separation of migrant families as inhumane and a violation of fundamental human rights. "It is an axiom of moral life among civilized humans that to separate young children from their parents is an offense against not just nature but society, one of the building blocks of which—as the Republican Party, in particular, has long been at pains to emphasize—is the family," Ashley Fetters wrote in the *Atlantic*. "Forcibly yanking children from their parents is of a piece with some of the darkest moments of American history: the internment of Japanese Americans; the forcible separation of American Indian children into special boarding schools; slavery" (Fetters 2019). In the face of public outrage and declining approval ratings, Trump signed an executive order rescinding the policy on June 20, 2018. The controversy continued over the next few months, however, as federal agencies failed to track the whereabouts of migrant children and struggled to reunite them with their families. In some instances, parents were deported without being able to locate or reclaim their children, who remained in the United States.

Even after Trump formally revoked the zero tolerance policy, immigration officials continued to detain large numbers of unaccompanied minors who entered the United States. Immigration attorneys, doctors, progressive lawmakers, journalists, and other observers who visited border detention facilities reported that migrant children were being held in overcrowded and unsanitary conditions without adequate supervision or access to basic necessities. They described children huddled in fenced enclosures, sleeping on concrete floors under thin Mylar blankets, dressed in filthy clothing, and lacking such hygiene items as soap and toothbrushes. The administration's treatment of migrant children received international condemnation, and medical experts predicted that minors subjected to such conditions would experience lasting psychological and physical harm. Trump blamed Democrats in Congress for not approving humanitarian funding to help CBP and other immigration agencies deal with an unprecedented influx of families and unaccompanied minors crossing the border.

The Border Crisis

Despite the Trump administration's efforts to close legal loopholes and deter migration, federal immigration agencies caught 851,500 people attempting to cross the U.S.–Mexico border in fiscal year 2019, including 474,000 families with children and 76,000 unaccompanied minors. The number of apprehensions more than doubled the 397,000 people arrested in 2018 and marked the highest total in a decade (Moore and Hauslohner 2019). Administration officials described the situation as a crisis and implemented further measures intended to eliminate incentives and stem the flow of migrants. One rule, for instance, required migrants to request asylum in the first safe country they entered, which enabled U.S. officials to reject applications from Central American migrants who passed through Mexico. The Migrant Protection Protocols—commonly known as the Remain in Mexico policy—required migrants to await U.S. immigration hearings in Mexican border towns, rather than in the United States.

Critics of Trump's immigration policies asserted that administration officials exaggerated the border crisis in order to justify harsh deterrent measures and pressure Congress to approve border-wall funding. Opponents pointed out that the number of people caught crossing the U.S.–Mexico border during Trump's presidency ranked low by historic standards, as apprehensions routinely surpassed 1 million per year from the 1980s through the early 2000s (Cadelago and Hesson 2018). Some critics argued that the administration's actions contributed to the crisis by restricting legal immigration channels, reducing refugee admissions, and narrowing the eligibility criteria for asylum. Immigrant rights advocates portrayed migration as a natural human response to poverty, famine, war, persecution, climate change, and other problems facing countries or regions. They recommended a humane approach to immigration that involved decriminalizing border crossing, expanding alternatives to detention, streamlining the asylum process, and bolstering efforts to help Central American nations provide their citizens with greater security and economic opportunity.

The Trump administration's aggressive response to the border crisis marked a new chapter in the long national debate over immigration. Supporters praised the president's approach as one that protected U.S. citizens from criminals and terrorists, preserved jobs, and promoted cultural unity. They viewed Trump as a strong leader whose bold policies secured the border and restricted immigration to the most deserving and desirable individuals. Opponents, on the other hand, accused the administration of human rights abuses and violations of international law protecting asylum seekers. Critics, such as Bloomberg opinion writer Noah Smith, claimed that Trump's words and actions generated fear, resentment, and bigotry toward immigrants and harmed the United States' international reputation as a humane, just, and hospitable nation. "So the American public (or at least those who determined the outcome of the Electoral College) got what it asked for," Smith said, "a president who was willing to brutalize poor desperate migrants and transform the U.S. into a much less welcoming country in exchange for a slight slowing of demographic change" (Smith 2019).

Further Reading

Cadelago, Christopher, and Ted Hesson. 2018. "Why Trump Is Talking Nonstop about the Migrant Caravan." *Politico*, October 23, 2018. https://www .politico.com/story/2018/10/23/trump-caravan-midterm-elections -875888.

Davis, Julie Hirschfeld, and Michael D. Shear. 2019. *Border Wars: Inside Trump's Assault on Immigration.* New York: Simon and Schuster.

Fetters, Ashley. 2019. "The Moral Failure of Family Separation." *Atlantic*, January 13, 2019. https://www.theatlantic.com/politics/archive/2019/01/trumps-family -separation-policy-causes-national-outrage/579676/.

Kamarck, Elaine, and Christine Stenglein. 2019. "Can Immigration Reform Happen? A Look Back." *Brookings*, February 11, 2019. https://www.brookings .edu/blog/fixgov/2019/02/11/can-immigration-reform-happen-a -look-back/.

Krikorian, Mark. 2008. "The New Case against Immigration." Center for Immigration Studies, July 18, 2008. http://www.cis.org/node/689.

Moore, Robert, and Abigail Hauslohner. 2019. "Trump Administration Working to Close Immigration 'Loopholes'—But Border Is Still a Crisis, Officials Say." *Washington Post*, October 30, 2019. https://www.washingtonpost.com /immigration/trump-administration-says-it-is-closing-immigration -loopholes-but-border-is-still-a-crisis/2019/10/29/99bbc9ac-fa62-11e9 -ac8c-8eced29ca6ef_story.html.

Obama, Barack. 2014. "Transcript of Obama's Immigration Speech." *Washington Post*, November 20, 2014. https://www.washingtonpost.com/politics /transcript-obamas-immigration-speech/2014/11/20/14ba8042-7117 -11e4-893f-86bd390a3340_story.html.

Smith, Noah. 2019. "The Southern Border Crisis Has Fizzled Out." Bloomberg, November 11, 2019. https://www.bloomberg.com/opinion/articles/2019-11 -11/the-southern-border-crisis-has-fizzled-out.

CHAPTER TWO

Landmark Events

This chapter explores important milestones and events in the contentious debate over immigration and border security in the United States. It discusses historic waves of immigration and major shifts in American attitudes and government policies toward immigrants, especially those crossing the U.S.–Mexico border. It then examines how Donald Trump rose to power by appealing to nativist sentiments in his 2016 presidential campaign, charts the immigration restrictions enacted by the Trump administration, and analyzes how Trump's enforcement policies led to the separation of migrant families and detention of migrant children at the southern border.

A Nation of Immigrants

The United States is often referred to as a nation of immigrants because it was founded and shaped by people whose ancestors came from other lands. "We call ourselves a nation of immigrants, and that's truly what we are," said President Ronald Reagan. "All of the immigrants who came to us brought their own music, literature, customs, and ideas. And the marvelous thing, a thing of which we're proud, is they did not have to relinquish these things in order to fit in. In fact, what they brought to America became American. And this diversity has more than enriched us; it has literally shaped us" (Riley 2008, ix).

Historians believe that the first human beings arrived in North America around 20,000 years ago, during the last Ice Age, by crossing the Bering Strait on a temporary land bridge. From there, these ancestors of modern Native Americans migrated across the continent, split into groups, and developed distinctive cultures as they adapted to their surroundings.

By the time European explorers began visiting the shores of North America in the 1400s, the aboriginal population had exceeded 1 million— although their numbers declined precipitously postcontact through epidemics of unfamiliar diseases, such as smallpox and measles.

When the explorers returned to Europe, their reports of the abundant land and resources available in the New World launched a wave of immigration. Hardy colonists from Great Britain, France, Spain, Sweden, and the Netherlands endured the dangerous, months-long Atlantic crossing in search of economic opportunity or religious freedom. They established small settlements along the east coast of North America, from modern-day New England to Florida, that grew into thriving communities by the early 1600s. In addition to free people who willingly made the journey to the New World, the growing population also included enslaved people who were forcibly transported from Africa. Historical records show that the first ship carrying enslaved Africans bound for the British North American colonies arrived in Jamestown, Virginia, in 1619. Over the next 250 years, an estimated half million more enslaved people were brought to America, where they were bought and sold as property and forced to work without pay.

The majority of early immigrants to North America hailed from Great Britain, which eventually organized 13 colonies stretching along the Atlantic Coast from Massachusetts to Georgia. Although the population began to diversify in the late 1600s with the arrival of immigrants from other European nations, English remained the dominant language and British laws and customs took hold. Over time, as colonists from different backgrounds and religions worked together to build a life in the New World, their cultures and traditions melded to create a distinctly American character. In 1776, the broadening gap between the colonists' outlook and the crown's priorities convinced the Americans to declare and fight for independence from British rule. The Revolutionary War concluded in 1783, when King George III signed the Treaty of Paris and formally recognized the United States of America as an independent nation.

In creating the U.S. Constitution and establishing a government, the leaders of the new nation made only a few minor legal distinctions between native-born American citizens and foreign-born people who became naturalized citizens of the United States. The Constitution guaranteed individual rights to all citizens—both American-born and naturalized—including the right to vote, run for elective office, and own property. However, it also specified that naturalized citizens were not eligible to serve as president or vice president of the United States. In 1790, Congress expanded the concept of birthright citizenship to include children born abroad to fathers who were U.S. citizens. Congress also passed legislation allowing foreign-born people to become naturalized citizens after they had resided in the United States for two years.

Waves of Immigration

The United States quickly gained a reputation as a land of freedom and opportunity—ideals that held strong appeal for people in Europe facing religious, ethnic, or political persecution. In addition, as Europe experienced trends toward greater industrialization and urbanization in the early 1800s, many large European cities struggled to cope with rapid population growth and such associated problems as poverty, pollution, and crime. Meanwhile, U.S. political and business leaders tended to look favorably upon immigration as a means of securing the nation's prosperity by providing a source of much-needed manpower to help develop its resources. They lured immigrants to America with the promise of lucrative factory jobs and ample farmland.

The combination of deteriorating conditions in Europe and boundless potential in America led to an upward trajectory in immigration to the United States during the 1800s. Nearly 1.75 million people arrived during the 1840s, up from a total of 600,000 during the 1820s and 1830s. Immigrants crowded into port cities along the eastern seaboard, with New York City receiving an average of 40 ships full of passengers each day. The new arrivals willingly endured danger, hardship, and uncertainty for the prospect of a better life. "Year by year, there were fewer alternatives until the critical day when only a single choice remained to be made—to emigrate or to die," immigration historian Oscar Handlin wrote in *The Uprooted* (Handlin 1951, 34).

Ireland produced an estimated one-third of all immigrants to the United States between 1820 and 1860. Prior to 1844, around 1 million Irish emigrated to escape overpopulation, poverty, or persecution for their Catholic faith. In 1845, a fungal disease known as blight devastated potato crops throughout Ireland, causing a widespread famine that killed 1.5 million people and prompted another 500,000 to flee to the United States. By 1850, New York City contained more Irish-born residents than Ireland's capital city of Dublin. Although Irish immigrants faced obstacles in America—including poverty, a lack of education, and discrimination on the basis of their Catholic faith—they also had the advantage of speaking English. Many Irish workers found jobs in factories, mills, and shipyards, and they used their large numbers to gain political influence.

Another major wave of immigrants to the United States during this period hailed from Germany. Political oppression, land shortages, and poor economic conditions encouraged around 5 million Germans to emigrate to America between 1820 and 1860. The new arrivals included many intellectuals, professionals, and skilled craftsmen. Rather than remaining in large cities along the Atlantic Coast, German immigrants established farms and businesses throughout the Midwest, forming German-speaking enclaves in such cities as Cincinnati, Milwaukee, Pittsburgh, and St. Louis. A large number of Chinese immigrants—primarily single men—arrived on the Pacific Coast beginning in 1849 with the discovery of gold in California. Chinese workers played an important role in constructing railroad lines and establishing small service businesses, such as restaurants and laundries.

The Civil War (1861–1865) years saw immigration to the United States slow to a trickle. The end of the war brought the abolition of slavery as well as the ratification of the Fourteenth Amendment to the Constitution, which granted full rights of citizenship to "all persons born or naturalized in the United States," including formerly enslaved persons. Following the postwar Reconstruction era, a massive new wave of immigration brought more than 20 million people to America between 1880 and 1920. In contrast to earlier arrivals, who came mainly from western and northern Europe, this wave consisted mostly of people from the southern, eastern, and central parts of the continent. The total included 4 million Italians as well as 2 million Jews from Russia, Austria-Hungary, and Romania. The advent of steam-powered passenger ships shortened the transatlantic passage considerably and facilitated their flight from poverty, political oppression, or religious persecution in their countries of origin.

Once they arrived in the United States, many people in the new wave of immigrants contributed to the trend toward urbanization and industrialization by settling in major cities and finding work in factories. The 1869 completion of the transcontinental railroad, however, encouraged many others to travel westward to establish farms, build towns, and develop natural resources by working in lumber mills, mines, or oil fields. During the 1870s, these immigrants competed with Chinese laborers for low-paying jobs, resulting in a tide of anti-Chinese racism, discrimination, and violence. In 1882, Congress responded to anti-Chinese hysteria by passing a blatantly racist immigration law. The Chinese Exclusion Act banned immigration by Chinese workers for ten years, prohibited Chinese immigrants from becoming naturalized citizens, and required Chinese people who left the United States to obtain certification prior to reentry.

Shifting Views of Immigrants

As early as colonial times, some Americans objected to unrestricted immigration. Opponents argued that the colonies should be reserved for people like themselves, who spoke English and shared the same beliefs and customs. They worried that allowing too many people from different backgrounds and cultures would change the character of the colonies and weaken their cohesion. At first, however, most Americans viewed immigration as a necessary means of acquiring the manpower needed to harvest natural resources and establish farms, cities, businesses, churches, and schools. Supporters argued that immigrants enriched the nation by contributing new talents and perspectives. They portrayed the United States as a "melting pot" for assimilating newcomers and incorporating the best elements of their cultures into a unified whole. "We are a nation of immigrants, but we are also a nation that loves to debate immigration policy and that's been true since day one," said immigration law professor Bill Ong Hing. "There's never going to be unanimity across the nation on what our immigration policy should be" (Campbell 2019).

The major waves of immigration often met with opposition from established Americans who viewed an influx of newcomers from one region or country as a threat to cherished traditions and ways of life. During the 1850s, for instance, the Know-Nothing political party arose in opposition to the arrival of large numbers of Irish Catholic immigrants, whom they portrayed as poor, uneducated, uncivilized, and subject to the pope's influence. By stirring up anti-Irish sentiments, the Know-Nothings gained 100 seats in Congress in 1854. Yet their 1856 presidential candidate, former president Millard Fillmore, only garnered eight electoral votes by running on an anti-immigration "Americans Must Rule America" platform, which included banning foreign-born and Catholic individuals from holding elected office and extending the residency requirement for becoming a naturalized U.S. citizen from 2 to 21 years. In contrast, Abraham Lincoln's victorious Republican Party platform of 1864 declared that "foreign immigration which in the past has added so much to the wealth, resources, and increase of power to the nation . . . should be fostered and encouraged by a liberal and just policy" (Moore and Harris 1996).

Anti-immigration sentiments arose again during the 1880s as a wave of immigrants began arriving from eastern and southern Europe. Some critics objected out of bigotry, claiming that these newcomers were inferior to people of western European ancestry and held radical political ideas. Although industrialists supported continued immigration as a source of cheap labor, many others expressed anxiety about the flood of unskilled immigrants, viewing them as a threat to wages, job security, social stability, and public health. Such feelings led to rising calls for the federal government to step in to regulate immigration. In the early 1890s, Senator Henry Cabot Lodge (R-MA) formed the Immigration Restriction League, which proposed subjecting would-be immigrants to literacy tests as a means of weeding out undesirable elements. "They wanted the complete exclusion of people different from themselves," said historian Michael McGerr. "Not content to let immigrants live apart in urban enclaves, these Americans . . . advocated immigration restrictions, a wall built around the United States" (McGerr 2003, 211).

By the late 1800s, even immigration supporters recognized the need for better record-keeping and regulation of the flood of people arriving daily in New York City and other ports on the East Coast. Prior to the enactment of immigration laws, new arrivals simply disembarked, passed through U.S. customs, and entered the country. In 1892, the federal government established Ellis Island in New York Harbor as an immigrant landing and processing station. Over the next six decades, 12 million people—or nearly three-quarters of all immigrants to the United States—passed through Ellis Island. As their ships approached, they were greeted by the Statue of Liberty—a 300-foot copper monument that had been dedicated in 1886 as a gift of friendship from France—which served as a symbol of hope, freedom, and democracy. The poem etched on the statue's base offered refuge to immigrants: "*Give me your tired, your poor, / Your huddled masses yearning to breathe free, / The wretched refuse of your teeming shore. / Send these, the homeless, tempest-tost to me, / I lift my lamp beside the golden door!*" (Lazarus 1883).

On Ellis Island, new arrivals underwent medical examinations and could be detained or turned away if they exhibited symptoms of such contagious diseases as favus (a fungal skin infection), trachoma (a bacterial eye infection), or tuberculosis (a bacterial lung infection). Immigration officials also conducted interviews to collect information about the age, gender, marital status, occupation, and country of origin for everyone entering the United States. People could be denied entry for having a criminal record or holding radical political views. Unaccompanied women often had to wait until a male sponsor came to escort them, and unmarried women with children were often rejected for immorality. People with disabilities or others who appeared likely to become dependent on public welfare were also turned away. Overall, however, immigration authorities only rejected about 2 percent of applicants at Ellis Island.

Efforts to Restrict Immigration

By the early twentieth century, the unprecedented flow of immigrants provoked a backlash and led to increased pressure for assimilation. More Americans came to resent new arrivals who sequestered themselves in ethnic neighborhoods and clung to the languages and customs of their countries of origin. "There is no room in this country for hyphenated Americanism," former president Theodore Roosevelt declared in a 1915 speech. "Our allegiance must be purely to the United States. We must unsparingly condemn any man who holds any other allegiance. But if he is heartily and singly loyal to this Republic, then no matter where he was born, he is just as good an American as anyone else" (Roosevelt 1915).

The outbreak of World War I (1914–1918) in Europe contributed to growing nationalist sentiments and suspicion toward foreigners. Feelings of resentment and animosity toward immigrants led to a surge in nativism—the desire to protect the interests of Americans of long standing (mainly white people from western or northern Europe) and preserve their cultural identity from outside influences. "The American people have come to sanction—indeed demand—reform of our immigration laws. They have seen, patent and plain, the encroachments of the foreign-born flood upon their own lives," said U.S. Representative Albert Johnson (R-WA). "The myth of the melting pot has been discredited. . . . The day of indiscriminate acceptance of all races has definitely ended" (Daniels 2004, 55).

These factors led to a series of efforts to restrict immigration to the United States. The Immigration Act of 1917, passed over President Woodrow Wilson's veto, expanded the Chinese Exclusion Act to ban immigrants from most of the Asia-Pacific region. It also instituted a literacy test that required all immigrants over age 16 to demonstrate the ability to read a short passage in their own language. Finally, the act featured an extensive list of categories of people who would be prohibited from entering the United States, including alcoholics, anarchists, beggars, convicts, idiots, insane persons, paupers, political radicals, polygamists, prostitutes, and vagrants (U.S. Congress 1917). In response to an influx of eastern European Jews fleeing persecution, Congress passed the Emergency Immigration Act of 1921. Also known as the Emergency Quota Act, it marked the first time that the federal government established numerical limits on European immigration. The legislation capped annual immigration from each country at 3 percent of the total number of foreign-born people of that nationality who had been recorded in the 1910 U.S. Census, which placed the total number of immigrant visas available at around 350,000 per year (Office of the Historian n.d.).

Congress passed the most sweeping immigration restrictions of the era with the Immigration Act of 1924, also known as the Johnson-Reed Act or the National Origins Act. The legislation reduced the quotas established three years earlier to 2 percent of each nationality recorded by the 1890 Census. This adjustment dramatically decreased the number of people admitted from southern and eastern Europe, since their resident population had been low prior to 1890, and favored people from northern and western Europe. In fact, the new quotas meant that 70 percent of the 150,000 annual immigrant visas went to applicants from Great Britain, Ireland, and Germany. The law also excluded immigrants from all of Asia except the Philippines, an American colony whose residents were considered U.S. citizens. The Immigration Act received support from labor unions, which sought to protect the jobs and wages of their members, as well as from individuals and groups who viewed certain classes of immigrants as inferior and sought to preserve the predominantly white racial composition of the United States.

The Immigration Act of 1924 launched a four-decade period of limited immigration to the United States. In addition to legal restrictions, such world events as the global economic depression of the 1930s and World War II (1939–1945) also served to reduce migration. As a result, the percentage of U.S. residents who were born in a different country declined from 11.6 percent of the population in 1930 to 6.9 percent in 1950 (Gibson and Jung 2007, 3). In response to the humanitarian crisis precipitated by the war in Europe, Congress passed the Displaced Persons Act of 1948, which enabled 400,000 refugees to be admitted to the United States over the next four years. Critics noted that Congress did not expand immigration quotas to accommodate these refugees—meaning that they took the place of other people who had been waiting for visas—and also charged that the admission criteria unfairly discriminated against Jewish refugees. In 1952, Congress passed the Immigration and Nationality Act, commonly known as the McCarran-Walter Act. In response to Cold War anticommunist fears, the legislation provided for increased screening of potential immigrants and added a "good moral character" requirement to the naturalization process. Although it reinforced the National Origins Quota System, it also created a preference system for family members of earlier immigrants and for people with special skills, education, or economic potential.

American attitudes toward immigration began to shift during the civil rights movement of the 1950s and 1960s, which placed a strong emphasis on racial equality and social justice. Congress responded by passing the Immigration and Nationality Act, also known as the Hart-Celler Act, which ended the longstanding quota system that had favored some racial and ethnic groups over others. Upon signing it into law, President Lyndon Johnson said it "corrects a cruel and enduring wrong in the conduct of the American Nation" (Johnson 1965). The legislation capped annual immigration at 290,000, with no more than 20,000 admitted from any one country, and established seven categories of preference that included family members of U.S. citizens, skilled immigrants, and people seeking asylum from religious, ethnic, or political persecution.

Although proponents of the new law claimed that it would not have a significant impact on the demographic composition of immigrants to the United States, it greatly reduced the number of visas available to people of European origin, who had made up the majority of immigrants to the United States prior to 1965. It also opened up immigration from regions that had been excluded or underrepresented in previous waves, including Latin America, Asia, Africa, and the Middle East. From 1971 to 1991, therefore, the majority of immigrants came from non-European backgrounds. People from Latin American nations made up nearly 48 percent of immigrants during that period, while people from Asia accounted for 35 percent.

Critics claim that the Hart-Celler Act also led to a surge in illegal immigration. They point out that the law's across-the-board annual cap of 20,000 immigrants per country, which was intended to make the system fair and unbiased, greatly expanded access to U.S. visas for residents of less populous nations while strictly limiting access for residents of more populous nations. In addition, the law failed to take geographic proximity and historic migration patterns into account when setting the cap. Prior to 1965, numerical limits on immigration to the United States had not applied to countries in the Western Hemisphere, so large numbers of migrant workers from nearby countries in Latin America had crossed the border in seasonal patterns. "When opportunities for legal entry closed up, the previous flows of immigrants were quickly re-established under unauthorized auspices," Douglas S. Massey wrote in the *Washington Post*. "Although little had changed in practical terms in the years after 1965— the same migrants were leaving the same communities to go to the same employers in the same U.S. states in about the same numbers—now the migrants were 'illegal' and hence by definition 'lawbreakers' and 'criminals'" (Massey 2015). As border security increased, more and more workers from Mexico and Central America decided to remain in the United States as undocumented immigrants. As a result, the 1965 law precipitated major changes in U.S. demographics, increasing the percentage of foreign-born people from 5 percent to 14 percent of the population over 50 years (Pew Research Center 2015), and led to new efforts to restrict immigration.

Further Reading

Campbell, Monica. 2019. "Trump's Immigration Policies Build on the History of Former U.S. Presidents." PRI's *The World*, July 12, 2019. https://www.pri.org /stories/2019-07-12/trumps-hard-line-immigration-policies-build -history-former-us-presidents.

Daniels, Roger. 2004. *Guarding the Golden Door: American Immigration Policy and Immigrants since 1882*. New York: Hill and Wang.

Gibson, Campbell, and Kay Jung. 2007. *The Foreign-Born Population of the United States, 1850–2000*. New York: Nova Science Publishers.

Handlin, Oscar. 1951. *The Uprooted*. Philadelphia: University of Pennsylvania Press.

Johnson, Lyndon B. 1965. "Remarks at the Signing of the Immigration Bill." Liberty Island, New York, LBJ Presidential Library, October 3, 1965. http://www.lbjlibrary.org/lyndon-baines-johnson/timeline/lbj-on-immigration.

Lazarus, Emma. 1883. "The New Colossus." Statue of Liberty National Monument, National Park Service, November 2, 1883. https://www.nps.gov /stli/learn/historyculture/colossus.htm.

Massey, Douglas S. 2015. "How a 1965 Immigration Reform Created Illegal Immigration." *Washington Post*, September 25, 2015. https://www.washingtonpost.com/posteverything/wp/2015/09/25/how-a-1965-immigration -reform-created-illegal-immigration/.

McGerr, Michael. 2003. *A Fierce Discontent: The Rise and Fall of the Progressive Movement in America*. New York: Oxford University Press.

Moore, Stephen, and Eric Harris. 1996. "Still the Pro-Immigration Party?" Cato Institute, August 26, 1996. https://www.cato.org/publications/commentary /still-proimmigration-party.

Office of the Historian. n.d. "The Immigration Act of 1924." U.S. Department of State. https://history.state.gov/milestones/1921-1936/immigration-act.

Pew Research Center. 2015. "Modern Immigration Wave Brings 59 Million to U.S., Driving Population Growth and Change through 2065." September 28, 2015. https://www.pewresearch.org/hispanic/2015/09/28/modern -immigration-wave-brings-59-million-to-u-s-driving-population-growth -and-change-through-2065/.

Riley, Jason L. 2008. *Let Them In: The Case for Open Borders*. New York: Gotham.

Roosevelt, Theodore. 1915. "Address to the Knights of Columbus." Carnegie Hall, New York, October 12, 1915. https://en.wikisource.org/wiki/Address_to _the_Knights_of_Columbus.

U.S. Congress. 1917. "An Act to Regulate the Immigration of Aliens to, and the Residence of Aliens in, the United States." Sixty-Fourth Congress, Session II, Chapter 29, February 5, 1917. http://library.uwb.edu/Static /USimmigration/39%20stat%20874.pdf.

History of Immigration at the Southern Border

Like the rest of North America, Mexico was populated by indigenous peoples for thousands of years before the arrival of European explorers. After Spain conquered the Aztec civilization in 1521, Mexico became a Spanish colony for the next three centuries, resulting in the mixture of indigenous and Spanish cultures. Mexicans first settled areas north of the Rio Grande that would eventually become the United States in the 1600s. The rugged deserts and mountains of northern Mexico remained sparsely populated, with a few small towns organized around mission churches, even after Mexico gained its independence from Spain in 1821. At that time, Mexican territory encompassed the present-day states of Arizona, California, Nevada, New Mexico, Texas, and Utah, as well as small sections of several other states.

As the United States expanded westward in the 1800s, American ranchers and settlers increasingly encroached upon Mexican territory and came into conflict with Mexico's government. In 1845, the U.S. government annexed Texas and granted it statehood. The following year, the ongoing territorial disputes escalated into the Mexican-American War (1846–1848), which ended in victory for the United States. When the two nations signed the Treaty of Guadalupe Hidalgo in 1848, Mexico ceded the northern half of its territory to the United States, which increased in size by one-third. In 1854, the United States acquired another slice of Mexican territory—in present-day southern Arizona and New Mexico—for $10 million through the Gadsden Purchase, which established the modern U.S.–Mexico border.

As the United States took over Mexican land, tens of thousands of Mexican citizens found themselves living in a different country. "The first Mexicans to become part of the United States never crossed any border," one historian explained. "Instead, the border crossed them" (Library of Congress n.d.). Under the Treaty of Guadalupe Hidalgo, most Mexican residents of the newly acquired territory became U.S. citizens and received the rights granted to citizens under the Constitution. The federal government struggled to enforce laws and protect property rights in the distant and rapidly developing West, however, so speculators quickly swooped in to deprive Mexican Americans of their desirable land. As a result, most migration across the border in the late 1800s involved ethnic Mexicans leaving the newly acquired U.S. territories and returning to Mexico.

Shifting Patterns in Mexican Immigration

Migration patterns began to shift in the early 1900s, when Mexican workers increasingly crossed the border seeking jobs in farming, ranching, and mining. The political upheaval and violence of the Mexican Revolution (1910–1920) produced a surge of Mexican immigrants to the United States, from around 20,000 per year in the 1910s to between 50,000 and 100,000 per year in the 1920s (Steinhauer and Young 2015). Many people crossed the Rio Grande between the cities of Ciudad Juárez in northern Mexico and El Paso in western Texas, which became known as the Ellis Island of the West. Although some Mexicans settled permanently in the United States, many others followed circular migration patterns, returning to their country of origin when they reached a certain level of earnings or when conditions in Mexico improved.

When Congress began passing restrictive immigration laws in the early twentieth century—including the Immigration Act of 1924, which established quotas based on national origin—they did not apply to Mexico or other countries in the Western Hemisphere. Agricultural concerns in the American Southwest pushed to exclude Mexican migrant workers from the quotas, arguing that they provided a cheap and reliable source of labor. In addition, federal officials tended to view Mexican immigrants as temporary additions to the workforce rather than permanent residents. In the absence of quotas restricting Mexican immigration, the 1930 U.S. Census recorded 600,000 Mexican-born people—three times the number counted in 1910.

The migration pattern reversed once again during the Great Depression of the 1930s. Facing widespread crop failures, food shortages, unemployment, and poverty, thousands of Mexican workers chose to return to Mexico. In addition, competition for scarce jobs and other resources created a hostile atmosphere for migrant workers. The federal government, as well as some state and municipal authorities, responded by launching "repatriation" programs aimed at convincing Mexican immigrants to leave the country. While some ethnic Mexicans willingly accepted offers of free train rides to the border, others—including some U.S. citizens—wound up being forcibly deported to Mexico.

During World War II, however, labor shortages in the agriculture industry led to increased demand for Mexican workers. In 1942, the U.S.

and Mexican governments negotiated the Mexican Farm Labor Agreement, which created the bracero program to bring Mexican contract laborers to the United States. The agreement specified that braceros would receive a minimum wage of 30 cents per hour and live in labor camps with adequate food, shelter, and sanitation. In many cases, though, they were paid very low wages and worked in grueling conditions. In fact, the Mexican government refused to send braceros to Texas for several years due to the poor treatment and discrimination they experienced. Mexican laborers proved so valuable to U.S. farming operations that the bracero program continued long after the war ended. By the time it concluded in 1964, more than 5 million Mexican braceros had worked in 24 states, and hundreds of thousands remained in the United States afterward. Many Mexican Americans moved from rural areas to urban areas in search of factory jobs. They formed thriving communities in many large cities, including Los Angeles, Chicago, New York, San Antonio, and Phoenix.

Growing Concerns about Illegal Immigration

In 1964, as part of a civil-rights era effort to make immigration laws more equitable, Congress abolished the quota system based on national origin and replaced it with an across-the-board annual limit of 20,000 immigrants per country. Since Mexico had been exempt from the quotas, this change significantly reduced the number of U.S. visas available to Mexican migrants each year. Critics contend that it thus precipitated an increase in illegal immigration, as Mexican workers maintained earlier patterns of migration across the border for jobs. In addition, when legal immigration channels closed, more Mexican immigrants chose to remain in the United States and brought their families across the border as well. As a result of both legal and illegal immigration, the number of Mexican-born people in the United States grew rapidly, from 576,000 in 1960 to 2.2 million in 1980 and to 4.3 million in 1990 (Migration Policy Institute 2017).

The growing presence of unauthorized immigrants in the United States made illegal immigration a major topic of political debate during the 1980s and 1990s. Congress attempted to address the problem by passing the Immigration Reform and Control Act (IRCA), also known as the Simpson-Mazzoli Act, which President Ronald Reagan signed into law in 1986. The law contained provisions aimed at increasing immigration enforcement by expanding patrols of the Mexican border and imposing penalties on employers that knowingly hired undocumented workers. It also attempted to "wipe the slate clean" on illegal immigration by granting amnesty and providing a path to citizenship for 3 million unauthorized immigrants already in the country. To qualify for amnesty, applicants had to reside in the United States continuously for five years, possess a clean criminal record, register for the military draft, and demonstrate basic knowledge of the English language and U.S. government and history. Mexican-born people accounted for 70 percent of the immigrants who gained legal permanent resident status through IRCA (Chishti, Meissner, and Bergeron 2011).

The passage of IRCA led to dramatic increases in immigration enforcement and border security during the 1990s and early 2000s. The number of border patrol agents grew from 3,600 in 1986 to 20,700 in 2011, for instance, while the annual funding appropriated to immigration agencies increased from $575 million to $17.2 billion over that 25-year period (Chishti, Meissner, and Bergeron 2011). Yet IRCA did not have the intended effect of decreasing illegal immigration to the United States. Instead, the number of migrants crossing the Mexican border without authorization continued to increase following its passage and proceeded at an estimated rate of 300,000 per year during the 1990s. In 2000, U.S. Border Patrol agents arrested 1.64 million people attempting to cross the southern border outside of legal points of entry, and 98 percent of those apprehended were Mexican nationals (Gonzalez-Barrera and Krogstad 2019). Critics claimed that the amnesty provisions of IRCA encouraged more people to cross the border illegally in hopes of eventually gaining legal status.

Immigration supporters argued that Mexican workers filled a need for low-paid, unskilled laborers in agriculture, construction, food service, hospitality, and other American industries. Many U.S. citizens and politicians resented undocumented immigrants, however, arguing that they took jobs and utilized services that rightfully belonged to Americans. Such concerns fueled a backlash in California, where 59 percent of voters approved Proposition 187, a 1994 ballot initiative that sought to deny undocumented people access to public education, nonemergency health services, and social welfare benefits. Although a federal court overturned the measure before it took effect, it spurred the U.S. Congress to pass new laws aimed at discouraging illegal immigration and forcing undocumented people to leave the country. The Illegal Immigration Reform and Immigrant Responsibility Act (IIRIRA), signed into law by President Bill Clinton in 1996, made it easier to arrest and deport noncitizens and authorized the construction of barriers along the U.S.–Mexico border. Meanwhile, the Personal Responsibility and Work Opportunity Reconciliation Act of 1996 made undocumented immigrants ineligible for federal welfare benefits, such as food stamps and Medicaid.

Despite such measures, the number of unauthorized Mexican immigrants in the United States continued to climb, reaching a peak of 6.9 million in 2007, compared to a total of 5.3 million unauthorized immigrants from all other countries. From 2007 onward, however, a combination of tougher enforcement and changing economic conditions created a situation in which more Mexican immigrants left the United States than entered it. More than 1 million Mexican families voluntarily returned to Mexico between 2009 and 2014, while immigration officials removed many others under the provisions of IIRIRA that simplified the deportation process (Radford 2019). By 2017, the number of unauthorized Mexican immigrants living in the United States decreased to 4.9 million—down 2 million from the peak level—and 83 percent had resided in the country for a decade or more (Gonzalez-Barrera and Krogstad 2019). Even though the rate of immigration has declined, a total of 11.2 million Mexican immigrants lived in the United States as of 2017, or about one-fourth of all immigrants in the country (Radford 2019). Mexican Americans held prominent positions in the realms of politics, government, business, entertainment, and the arts. In addition, many aspects of Mexican culture became integrated into American life, from food and language to holidays and music.

Further Reading

Chishti, Muzaffar, Doris Meissner, and Claire Bergeron. 2011. "At Its 25th Anniversary, IRCA's Legacy Lives On." Migration Policy Institute, November 16, 2011. https://www.migrationpolicy.org/article/its-25th-anniversary -ircas-legacy-lives.

Dungan, Ron. 2017. "A Moving Border, and the History of a Difficult Boundary." *USA Today*, 2017. https://www.usatoday.com/border-wall/story/us-mexico -border-history/510833001/.

Gonzalez-Barrera, Ana, and Jens Manuel Krogstad. 2019. "What We Know about Illegal Immigration from Mexico." Pew Research Center, June 28, 2019. https://www.pewresearch.org/fact-tank/2019/06/28/what-we-know -about-illegal-immigration-from-mexico/.

Library of Congress. n.d. "Mexican Immigration." American Memory Learning Page, http://www.loc.gov/teachers/classroommaterials/presentationsand activities/presentations/immigration/mexican.html.

Migration Policy Institute. 2017. "Mexican-Born Population Over Time, 1850-Present." 2017. https://www.migrationpolicy.org/programs/data-hub /us-immigration-trends#history.

Radford, Jynnah. 2019. "Key Findings about U.S. Immigrants." Pew Research Center, June 17, 2019. https://www.pewresearch.org/fact-tank/2019/06 /17/key-findings-about-u-s-immigrants/.

Steinhauer, Jason, and Julia Young. 2015. "How Mexican Immigration to the United States Has Evolved." *Time*, March 12, 2015. https://time.com /3742067/history-mexican-immigration/.

Trends in Immigration and Enforcement (2000–2016)

When President Ronald Reagan signed the Immigration Reform and Control Act into law in 1986, few observers expected that it would represent the last major overhaul of U.S. immigration policy for decades. Although immigration remained a subject of intense political debate, the increasing polarization of American politics and public opinion prevented the passage of any meaningful immigration reform legislation through 2019. "In 33 years, the country has gone from the ability to forge a bipartisan consensus on immigration to a state of gridlock," wrote Brookings Institution scholars Elaine Kamarck and Christine Stenglein. "By 2007 both parties had to confront the reality they live with today: immigration has become intricately bound up with issues of identity, prone to the politics of tribalism, and of less interest to the business community" (Kamarck and Stenglein 2019). Although bipartisan solutions proved elusive, immigration reform remained a high priority for presidential administrations in the twenty-first century.

Immigration Policy under George W. Bush

Before taking office in 2001, President George W. Bush served as the Republican governor of Texas, which shares a 1,250-mile border with Mexico that features 28 legal points of entry. Since Texas was once part of Mexico and has a large and influential Latino population, Bush held more nuanced views of immigration than some of his fellow Republicans. Although he expressed support for strict border enforcement to prevent illegal immigration, he also praised the contributions of Mexican Americans and other immigrants to American life. "We are a nation of laws, and we must enforce our laws. We're also a nation of immigrants, and we must uphold that tradition, which has strengthened our country in so many ways," he stated. "These are not contradictory goals. America can be a lawful society and a welcoming society at the same time" (Bush 2006).

The federal government's approach to immigration changed following the terrorist attacks against the United States on September 11, 2001. Rather than viewing immigration as a social and economic issue, policymakers increasingly saw it as a national security issue. Since the foreign-born perpetrators of the attacks entered the United States legally on tourist, business, or student visas, lawmakers debated measures to prevent potential terrorists from gaining entry to the country in the future. Less than two months after the attacks, Congress passed the USA Patriot Act, which expanded the authority of law enforcement agencies to monitor, detain, and deport foreigners based on suspicion of terrorist activity or affiliation with terrorist groups. In 2002, Congress integrated 22 federal agencies into the Department of Homeland Security (DHS). The newly created, Cabinet-level department assumed responsibility for securing the nation against all manner of threats it might face, including counterterrorism, cybersecurity, disaster preparedness, emergency response, and protection of critical infrastructure.

DHS was also charged with overseeing the security of U.S. borders, including overland, maritime, and aviation approaches. Three DHS agencies played roles in border security and immigration enforcement: U.S. Citizenship and Immigration Services (CIS), which processed applications for asylum, residency, and citizenship; U.S. Customs and Border Protection (CBP), which patrolled borders and enforced immigration and customs laws; and U.S. Immigration and Customs Enforcement (ICE), which investigated violations of immigration laws and handled detention, removal, and deportation activities. These three agencies took over the former duties of the Immigration and Naturalization Service (INS), which the legislation abolished. Bush thus achieved his goal of dividing responsibility for the administration of legal immigration requests and the enforcement of immigration laws among separate agencies.

During Bush's two terms in office, he doubled federal funding for border security, from $4.6 billion in 2001 to $10.4 billion in 2007. He also increased the number of border patrol agents from 9,000 to 15,000 over this same period and sent 6,000 National Guard members to assist security efforts at the southern border by installing fences and operating surveillance systems (Bush 2007). Using the expanded authority of the USA Patriot Act, the Bush administration also deported a total of 10 million noncitizens from the United States. Approximately 8 million of these people were classified as "returns," meaning that they were either turned away at the border or voluntarily left the country through an informal administrative process, without facing legal penalties. The remaining 2 million people were classified as "removals," meaning that a judge found them to be in violation of immigration laws and issued a formal order of deportation, which carries legal consequences that include ineligibility to return to the United States for a number of years. DHS also expanded its detention facilities for undocumented immigrants under Bush and created an electronic database to identify aliens who were arrested or incarcerated.

Despite these measures, the number of undocumented immigrants residing in the United States increased significantly during Bush's presidency, from 8.6 million in 2000 to a peak of 12.2 million—or 4 percent of the U.S. population—in 2007 (Krogstad, Passel, and Cohn 2019). As a result, Bush's immigration policies came under intense criticism. Many conservative Republicans claimed that the 8.2 million undocumented immigrants in the workforce in 2007 reduced the job security and wages of American workers, and some called for mass deportation of people who entered the country illegally. Although Bush opposed amnesty programs and automatic paths to citizenship for undocumented immigrants, he also argued that mass deportation was unwise and unrealistic. Instead, he expressed support for a "rational middle ground" approach that required undocumented workers to pay a penalty for their illegal conduct, find steady employment, pay taxes, pass a criminal background check, learn English, and wait in line behind legal applicants before they became eligible for citizenship.

Bush also proposed establishing a temporary guest worker program to enable American business interests to employ low-cost immigrant labor. He emphasized that increased border security could not prevent all undocumented workers from entering the United States in search of jobs and a better life. He argued that creating a legal channel for employment of temporary guest workers could boost the U.S. economy as well as benefit foreign workers and reduce illegal immigration. "I propose a new temporary-worker program to match willing foreign workers with willing employers when no Americans can be found to fill the job," Bush said in his 2004 State of the Union address. "This reform will be good for our economy, because employers will find needed workers in an honest and orderly system. A temporary-worker program will help protect our homeland, allowing border patrol and law enforcement to focus on true threats to our national security" (Bush 2004). To prevent cheating, Bush promised to implement "tamperproof" identification cards to help employers verify the status of legal foreign workers, as well as to tighten worksite enforcement and hold employers accountable for hiring undocumented workers.

Bush made several attempts to convince Congress to pass a comprehensive immigration reform bill. In 2007, when the number of undocumented immigrants in the United States exceeded 12 million, he spoke about the need for a coordinated approach. "We must address the problem of illegal immigration and deliver a system that is secure, productive, orderly, and fair," Bush stated. "All elements of this problem must be addressed together—or none of them will be solved" (Bush 2007).

Although the Secure Borders, Economic Opportunity, and Immigration Reform Act of 2007 received vigorous debate in the 110th U.S. Congress, the legislation stalled out before passage. Pro-immigration groups objected to provisions that increased funding for border enforcement, while anti-immigration groups criticized provisions that granted legal status and established an eventual path to citizenship for undocumented immigrants.

Immigration Policy under Barack Obama

By the time Democrat Barack Obama took office as the 44th president of the United States in 2009, the country was mired in a severe economic recession. The lack of jobs and economic opportunity led to a steep decline in the number of people seeking to enter the United States illegally. In fact, more undocumented immigrants left the country than arrived during the downturn, resulting in a decrease in the unauthorized population to 11.4 million in 2010 (Krogstad, Passel, and Cohn 2019). Obama hoped to take advantage of this shift to garner bipartisan support for passage of a comprehensive immigration reform bill. He proposed to overhaul the existing system to improve border and worksite enforcement, adjust immigration figures to match economic conditions, offer a path to citizenship for long-settled undocumented immigrants, and increase funding for immigrant resettlement and assimilation programs.

To convince Republicans in Congress to support his plan, Obama sought to demonstrate his commitment to maintaining border security and preventing illegal immigration. His initial approach involved stepping up efforts to identify, locate, and deport undocumented immigrants who met certain conditions. Obama established enforcement priorities for ICE and CBP that focused, first and foremost, on removing potential terrorists, violent criminals, drug traffickers, gang members, and other individuals who threatened national security or public safety. Obama also prioritized the apprehension and removal of recent arrivals to the United States and repeat violators of U.S. immigration laws. Administration officials argued that these priorities put limited enforcement resources to the most productive use. Immigrant advocates also noted that targeting criminals and recent arrivals reduced the likelihood of deporting undocumented immigrants who had lived in the United States for many years and established homes, families, businesses, and roots in their communities.

In practice, the Obama administration's immigration enforcement scheme did not always work as intended. Targeting criminals sometimes meant deporting long-term residents who committed minor infractions, such as driving without a license. Similarly, targeting recent arrivals and repeat offenders sometimes meant deporting people with roots in the United States who overstayed a visa or attempted to reenter the country after a prior order of deportation. Overall, the number of deportations reached record levels during the early years of Obama's presidency. In 2011, ICE removed nearly 397,000 immigrants, with 55 percent having been convicted of crimes ranging from homicide to driving under the influence (Barnett 2011). In 2014, Obama issued an executive order clarifying the priorities for ICE, which raised the proportion of removals who had been convicted of a serious crime to 91 percent (Marshall 2016).

Critics pointed out that Obama deported more than 2.5 million people during his time in office, prompting some immigrant rights advocates to dub him the "deporter in chief." Joanne Lin, a lawyer for the American Civil Liberties Union (ACLU), argued that mass deportations wasted taxpayer money and devastated Latino communities across the United States. "These record-breaking deportation numbers come at a time when illegal immigration rates have plummeted, the undocumented population has decreased substantially, and violent crime rates are at their lowest levels in 40 years," she said. Obama's secretary of Homeland Security, Janet Napolitano, insisted that the administration did a better job than previous administrations of targeting undesirable immigrants for deportation while protecting law-abiding immigrants. "What . . . critics will ignore is that while the overall number of individuals removed will exceed prior years, the composition of that number will have fundamentally changed," she declared (Barnett 2011).

Some administration officials claimed that the deportation numbers seemed inflated because Obama's policies resulted in a larger percentage of immigrants being subjected to compulsory removals rather voluntary returns. While Obama removed more immigrants than his predecessors, his combined figures for removals and returns—at 5 million—ranked lower than those of presidents George W. Bush (10 million) and Bill Clinton (12 million). "A straight numbers-by-numbers comparison doesn't provide an accurate picture of what was going on in the administration," said Cecilia Muñoz, a top immigration policy adviser to Obama. "It is more humane to be removing people who have been here two weeks than it is to be removing people who have been here for 20 years and have families" (Wolf 2019).

Obama's push for comprehensive immigration reform produced results in the Senate, which passed the Border Security, Economic Opportunity, and Immigration Modernization Act in June 2013 by a solid 68–32 vote.

The Senate bill proposed providing a path to citizenship for most unauthorized immigrants, allocating $46 billion to increase the number of border patrol agents and install fencing on the border, strengthening worksite enforcement and visa tracking systems, and implementing a point system to evaluate applicants for immigration. Speaker John Boehner refused to bring the bill up for a vote in the House, however, saying that his Republican colleagues did not trust Obama on the immigration issue.

When it became clear that the bipartisan immigration reform legislation would not pass, Obama announced plans to enact new immigration policies unilaterally through a series of executive orders. "Today, our immigration system is broken, and everybody knows it," he said. "Families who enter our country the right way and play by the rules watch others flout the rules. Business owners who offer their workers good wages and benefits see the competition exploit undocumented immigrants by paying them far less. All of us take offense to anyone who reaps the rewards of living in America without taking on the responsibilities of living in America. And undocumented immigrants who desperately want to embrace those responsibilities see little option but to remain in the shadows, or risk their families being torn apart" (Obama 2014).

In 2012, Obama had issued an executive order establishing the Deferred Action for Childhood Arrivals (DACA) program, which allowed an estimated 700,000 immigrants who were brought to the United States illegally as children prior to 2010 to receive work permits and temporary, renewable deferments from deportation. His 2014 executive actions extended DACA protection to 270,000 more immigrants who entered the country as children but were currently over age 30. In addition, his Deferred Action for Parents of Americans and Lawful Permanent Residents (DAPA) program extended protection from deportation to around 4 million more unauthorized immigrants who had been in the country at least five years and were parents of U.S. citizens or legal immigrants. In total, the executive actions would have granted temporary legal status to nearly half of all undocumented immigrants residing in the United States, but a court injunction prevented them from taking effect.

Obama faced an immigration crisis in 2014, when more than 60,000 unaccompanied migrant children attempted to cross the U.S.–Mexico border. This figure represented a tenfold increase from 2011, and the sudden surge overwhelmed the personnel and resources available to process, transport, feed, and shelter them. The majority of the unaccompanied minors were teenagers fleeing from poverty, corruption, gang violence, or domestic abuse in the Northern Triangle countries of Central America—El Salvador, Guatemala, and Honduras. Some of them hoped to reunite with parents or other relatives already living as undocumented immigrants in the United States. Critics blamed the influx on the DACA program and other Obama policies that shielded undocumented immigrants. "Obama's administration blasted a range of loopholes that, collectively, incentivized illegal immigration, no doubt about it," said Dan Stein, president of the Federation for American Immigration Reform (Rose 2019).

Several laws and court rulings restricted the federal government's handling of unaccompanied migrant children in custody. The William Wilberforce Trafficking Victims Protection Reauthorization Act of 2008, for instance, established special rules for returning unaccompanied children to noncontiguous countries that did not share a border with the United States. These rules required children to receive formal removal hearings in immigration courts, which could take months or even years. In the meantime, they had to be released from CBP detention and placed in the "least restrictive setting possible"—with relatives or sponsors or in foster homes or shelters—while their cases were pending. The legal standards for the treatment of unaccompanied migrant children while in CBP custody were established in 1997 by the Flores Settlement Agreement (FSA). The terms of the FSA required federal authorities to house minors in "safe and sanitary" facilities, give them access to basic necessities, and make "prompt and continuous" efforts to reunite them with family members.

The sheer numbers of migrant children and families crossing the southern border made it difficult and expensive for the Obama administration to comply with these rules. Obama requested an emergency appropriation of $4 billion to build additional facilities and hire more personnel to address the crisis. He also sought changes to the law to make it easier to process the large numbers of minors attempting to enter the United States. In 2015, the administration asked a federal court to modify the FSA to allow immigration agencies to detain migrant children with their parents while their asylum applications were processed. District Court Judge Dolly Gee denied the request. In doing so, she ruled that the FSA requirements applied to children who entered the United States as part of family units as well as to unaccompanied minors. She also interpreted the FSA's stipulation that the government must release children from detention "without unnecessary delay" to mean 20 days.

In effect, the ruling forced immigration authorities to release entire migrant families within 20 days to remain in compliance with the FSA. Although the court did not require adult family members to be released from detention, the Obama administration adopted a practice of releasing families together to avoid separating children from their parents. The only exceptions came when immigration officials deemed the parents unsuitable to care for the children, usually because they had a criminal record or had committed domestic abuse. Critics referred to this policy as "catch and release." They claimed that most people treated with such leniency never appeared for their asylum hearings and instead joined the large population of undocumented immigrants residing in the United States. Furthermore, they argued that the policy encouraged parents—as well as unrelated adults, such as smugglers and human traffickers—to bring children across the border illegally.

Further Reading

Barnett, Jim. 2011. "U.S. Deportations Reach Historic Levels." CNN, October 18, 2011. https://www.cnn.com/2011/10/18/us/immigrant-deportations/.

Bush, George W. 2004. "State of the Union." White House, January 20, 2004. https://georgewbush-whitehouse.archives.gov/stateoftheunion/2004/.

Bush, George W. 2006. "Bush's Speech on Immigration." *New York Times*, May 15, 2006. https://www.nytimes.com/2006/05/15/washington/15text-bush.html.

Bush, George W. 2007. "President Bush's Plan for Comprehensive Immigration Reform." White House, 2007. https://georgewbush-whitehouse.archives .gov/stateoftheunion/2007/initiatives/immigration.html.

Cowan, Richard. 2014. "Waves of Immigrant Minors Present Crisis for Obama, Congress." *Reuters*, May 28, 2014. https://www.reuters.com/article/us-usa -immigration-children/waves-of-immigrant-minors-present-crisis -for-obama-congress-idUSKBN0E814T20140528.

Editorial Board. 2019. "All Presidents Are Deporters in Chief." *New York Times*, July 13, 2019. https://www.nytimes.com/2019/07/13/opinion/sunday/trump -deportations-immigration.html.

Hing, Bill Ong. 2018. *American Presidents, Deportations, and Human Rights Violations: From Carter to Trump.* New York: Cambridge University Press.

Kamarck, Elaine, and Christine Stenglein. 2019. "Can Immigration Reform Happen? A Look Back." *Brookings*, February 11, 2019. https://www.brookings .edu/blog/fixgov/2019/02/11/can-immigration-reform-happen-a -look-back/.

Krogstad, Jens Manuel, Jeffrey S. Passel, and D'Vera Cohn. 2019. "5 Facts about Illegal Immigration in the U.S." Pew Research Center, June 12, 2019. https://www.pewresearch.org/fact-tank/2019/06/12/5-facts-about -illegal-immigration-in-the-u-s/.

Lind, Dara. 2018. "What Obama Did with Migrant Families vs. What Trump Is Doing." Vox, June 21, 2018. https://www.vox.com/2018/6/21/17488458 /obama-immigration-policy-family-separation-border.

Marshall, Serena. 2016. "Obama Has Deported More People Than Any Other President." ABC News, August 29, 2016. https://abcnews.go.com/Politics /obamas-deportation-policy-numbers/story?id=41715661.

Obama, Barack. 2014. "Transcript of Obama's Immigration Speech." *Washington Post*, November 20, 2014. https://www.washingtonpost.com/politics /transcript-obamas-immigration-speech/2014/11/20/14ba8042 -7117-11e4-893f-86bd390a3340_story.html.

Rose, Joel. 2019. "President Obama Also Faced a 'Crisis' at the Southern Border." NPR, January 9, 2019. https://www.npr.org/2019/01/09/683623555 /president-obama-also-faced-a-crisis-at-the-southern-border.

Wolf, Zachary B. 2019. "Yes, Obama Deported More People Than Trump, but Context Is Everything." CNN, July 13, 2019. https://www.cnn.com/2019/07/13 /politics/obama-trump-deportations-illegal-immigration/index.html.

Yglesias, Matthew. 2019. "The Weird Controversy over Democrats 'Criticizing Obama' at This Week's Debate, Explained." Vox, August 2, 2019. https:// www.vox.com/policy-and-politics/2019/8/2/20751676/democrats -debate-criticizing-obama-immigration.

Donald Trump's Immigration Policies (2016–)

From the time he announced his candidacy for the Republican presidential nomination in 2015, businessman Donald Trump made immigration policy a centerpiece of his campaign. His hardline stance on the issue represented a significant departure from the more nuanced approaches adopted by previous administrations—both Democratic and Republican—dating back three decades. Trump's predecessors tended to embrace legal immigration as an important part of America's "melting pot" heritage, arguing that it enriched the nation with new and diverse ideas, talents, and traditions. They typically portrayed legal immigration as a social and economic good while using targeted enforcement to control illegal immigration in a fair and humane manner.

Trump, on the other hand, framed both legal and illegal immigration as threats to national security, public safety, and the U.S. economy. He argued that the lenient immigration policies pursued by previous administrations had harmed American workers and contributed to an increase in violent crime. "We have to listen to the concerns that working people, our forgotten working people, have over the record pace of immigration and its impact on their jobs, wages, housing, schools, tax bills, and general living conditions," he declared in an August 2016 campaign speech. "We will terminate the Obama administration's deadly, and it is deadly, non-enforcement policies that allow thousands of criminal aliens to freely roam our streets, walk around, do whatever they want to do, crime all over the place" (Trump 2016).

Trump also asserted that decades of uncontrolled immigration had negatively impacted the nation's demographic makeup and cultural unity. Echoing some xenophobic anti-immigrant crusades of the past, he portrayed some immigrants—particularly Latino immigrants from Mexico and Central America and Muslim immigrants from the Middle East—as undesirable or even dangerous. "We also have to be honest about the fact that not everyone who seeks to join our country will be able to successfully assimilate," he declared. "It's our right, as a sovereign nation, to choose immigrants that we think are the likeliest to thrive and flourish and love us" (Trump 2016). Trump promised to reform the legal immigration system to "keep immigration levels measured by population share within historical norms" and to "select immigrants based on their likelihood of success in U.S. society and their ability to be financially self-sufficient" (Trump 2016). He also promised to aggressively enforce U.S. immigration laws to halt illegal immigration and force undocumented immigrants to leave the country.

Border Security and Enforcement

The signature issue of Trump's anti-immigration campaign involved his promise to build a wall extending along the entire 1,900-mile length of the U.S.–Mexico border. He described the wall as necessary to secure the southern border and prevent illegal crossings. "On day one, we will begin working on an impenetrable, physical, tall, powerful, beautiful southern border wall," he stated. "And Mexico will pay for the wall. One hundred percent. They don't know it yet, but they're going to pay for it" (Trump 2016). Once he took office in January 2017, however, Trump struggled to turn his vision of a border wall into reality. He encountered opposition from private landowners reluctant to break up their property, environmental groups critical of the potential impact on ecosystems and migratory species, engineers who questioned the feasibility of the project, and the Mexican government, which repeatedly denied any intention of funding it. Most importantly, Congress refused to appropriate the billions of dollars Trump demanded to build the wall. By August 2019—two and a half years into Trump's term—U.S. Customs and Border Protection (CBP) had replaced about 60 miles of dilapidated fencing within the 650 miles of primary barriers that already existed along the border when he took office (Valverde 2019). But Trump had made virtually no progress on his promises to extend a new wall the entire length of the border and to make Mexico pay for it.

Trump also promised to eliminate loopholes in immigration enforcement that he claimed allowed dangerous gang members, drug dealers, human traffickers, and other criminals to enter and remain in the United States. Throughout his presidential campaign, Trump consistently portrayed immigrants as criminals and immigration as a threat to public safety and national security. At his 2015 campaign launch event, for instance, he made a controversial statement equating Mexican migrants with rapists. "When Mexico sends its people, they're not sending their best," he said. "They're sending people that have lots of problems, and they're bringing those problems with us. They're bringing drugs. They're bringing crime. They're rapists. And some, I assume, are good people" (Phillips 2017). Trump also blamed immigrants for high crime rates in American cities and preventable deaths of American citizens. "Countless innocent American lives have been stolen because our politicians have failed in their duty to secure our borders and enforce our laws like they have to be enforced," he stated. "I have met with many of the great parents who lost their children to sanctuary cities and open borders" (Trump 2016).

Immigrant rights advocates challenged the idea that immigrants brought violence and crime to American cities. A major study of 300 metropolitan areas found that while the immigrant population increased by 137 percent between 1980 and 2016, on average, crime rates fell by 12 percent over the same period (Flagg 2018). Other studies showed that undocumented immigrants were 50 percent less likely to be incarcerated than native-born Americans, while legal immigrants were 80 percent less likely (Haslett 2019). Some analysts suggested that a fear of deportation contributed to lower crime rates among undocumented immigrants.

Trump continued to use inflammatory rhetoric about immigrants and crime after he took office. A *USA Today* analysis found that he used such terms as "alien," "animal," "criminal," "invasion," "killer," and "predator" more than 500 times while discussing immigration and border security at rallies (Fritze 2019). Immigrant rights advocates asserted that such terms served to dehumanize migrants from Central America and Mexico—many of whom sought asylum in the United States to escape persecution and violence in their home countries—and stoke fear and hatred toward immigrants among Americans. "The use of repetition—a propaganda mainstay—points to an intention by Trump to impose a way of thinking about his designated targets," said history professor Ruth Ben-Ghiat (Fritze 2019). Some critics claimed that Trump's terminology incited violence. In August 2019, a white nationalist who told authorities he was "targeting Mexicans" killed 22 people in a mass shooting at a Walmart store in El Paso. In an online manifesto, the gunman echoed Trump's anti-immigrant rhetoric by describing the attack as "a response to the Hispanic invasion of Texas" (Arce 2019).

Trump used his assertions about immigrants and crime to justify aggressive policies aimed at deporting undocumented immigrants. He promised to triple the number of ICE deportation officers and to "create a new special deportation task force focused on identifying and quickly removing the most dangerous criminal illegal immigrants in America who have evaded justice" (Trump 2016). He also vowed to withhold federal funding from so-called sanctuary cities that refused to cooperate with ICE, and to force foreign governments to take custody of their citizens who received deportation orders from the United States due to criminal activity.

Of the 11 million undocumented immigrants in the United States, Trump claimed that at least 2 million had criminal records, although he did not differentiate between arrests and convictions or specify whether the offenses were felonies or misdemeanors (Haslett 2019). "Our enforcement priorities will include removing criminals, gang members, security threats, visa overstays, public charges," Trump declared. "That is those relying on public welfare or straining the safety net along with millions of recent illegal arrivals and overstays who've come here under this current corrupt [Obama] administration" (Trump 2016). In practice, however, the Trump administration applied less discriminating standards to remove undocumented immigrants. Only 3 percent of the Trump administration's fiscal 2019 removal requests cited criminal activity, compared to about 50 percent of removals under Obama (Bump 2019).

Trump acknowledged that his ultimate goal was to force all undocumented immigrants to leave the United States because they had all broken the law by entering the country illegally. "For those here illegally today, who are seeking legal status, they will have one route and one route only. To return home and apply for reentry like everybody else," he stated. "There will be no amnesty. Our message to the world will be this. You cannot obtain legal status or become a citizen of the United States by illegally entering our country. . . . People will know that you can't just smuggle in, hunker down, and wait to be legalized. It's not going to work that way. Those days are over" (Trump 2016).

As part of his commitment to eliminating amnesty options for undocumented immigrants, Trump threatened to rescind the Deferred Action for Childhood Arrivals (DACA) program—an Obama-era policy that enabled an estimated 700,000 young people who had been brought to the United States illegally as children to work and go to school without fear of deportation—which he described as an unconstitutional executive action.

In the fall of 2017, the federal government announced that it would stop granting DACA benefits to new applicants and issuing renewals to DACA recipients whose benefits expired. A federal judge issued a nationwide injunction shortly before the change took effect, however, which prevented more than 900 immigrants from losing their DACA protections each day (Pierce, Bolter, and Selee 2018).

Finally, Trump promised to crack down on businesses that employed undocumented workers in order to eliminate financial incentives for people to cross the border illegally. In January 2018, ICE conducted a series of coordinated raids on nearly a hundred 7-Eleven convenience stores nationwide and arrested dozens of workers suspected of lacking legal status. In the biggest enforcement effort to date, ICE raided chicken processing plants in Mississippi in August 2019 and arrested nearly 700 people. Critics argued that undocumented immigrants mainly performed jobs that native-born Americans did not want. They claimed that these enforcement actions ripped apart families, caused fear and anxiety in immigrant communities, and worsened a national labor shortage for low-skilled workers. Immigrant rights advocates also pointed out that two-thirds of all unauthorized immigrants had resided in the United States for more than a decade as of 2017 (Krogstad, Passel, and Cohn 2019), making it likely that they had established homes and businesses, raised families, paid taxes, formed deep roots in their communities, and maintained few connections to their countries of origin.

Immigration Restrictions

In addition to stepping up enforcement to prevent illegal immigration, Trump also sought to restrict legal immigration. "We've admitted 59 million immigrants to the United States between 1965 and 2015. Many of these arrivals have greatly enriched our country," he said. "But we now have an obligation to them and to their children to control future immigration" (Trump 2016). Trump proposed ending "chain migration," for instance, by eliminating longstanding rules that allowed U.S. citizens to sponsor immediate family members for legal immigration. He also suggested throwing out the "visa lottery"—formally the Diversity Immigrant Visa program, established under the Immigration Act of 1990—which set aside 55,000 visas annually for applicants from countries that sent low numbers of immigrants to the United States over the preceding five years. Citing these as examples of "sick, demented laws that have to be changed," Trump said they favored immigrants who "are not the people that we want" (Kwong 2019). In 2018, however, First Lady Melania Trump's parents became U.S. citizens after she sponsored their legal immigration from Slovenia through the "chain migration" process.

Immediately after taking office, Trump followed through on his promise to suspend the issuance of visas to countries that he felt did not conduct adequate screening of applicants. In January 2017, he signed Executive Order 13769, which established a "travel ban" that temporarily halted immigration and restricted travel to the United States by citizens of seven predominantly Muslim nations (Iran, Iraq, Libya, Somalia, Sudan, Syria, and Yemen). Trump claimed that this controversial measure was necessary to prevent potential terrorists from entering the country. Opponents launched several lawsuits challenging the ban, arguing that it unfairly discriminated against Muslims and violated constitutional guarantees of religious liberty. The courts agreed and overturned it, citing statements Trump made during the campaign "calling for a total and complete shutdown of Muslims entering the United States" and claiming "there is great hatred towards Americans by large segments of the Muslim population" (Bier 2017).

Trump subsequently revised the executive order twice before the U.S. Supreme Court in June 2018 upheld a version that restricted entry by people from Iran, Libya, Somalia, Syria, Yemen, North Korea, and Venezuela. Although the first five nations had predominantly Muslim populations, the majority opinion found that the administration based the ban on legitimate national security concerns rather than on religious hostility. By September 2019, the travel ban had resulted in more than 31,300 applicants being refused visas to enter the United States. The State Department also granted 7,600 waivers or exceptions, although that number amounted to less than 6 percent of requests (Alvarez 2019). Thousands of other applications remained mired in the Trump administration's "extreme vetting" process, resulting in the long-term separation of many couples and families. Critics derided the ban as outright religious discrimination and argued that it did nothing to increase national security. "The Muslim ban has not made us safer," said Representative Jerry Nadler (D-NY). "It has weakened our standing in the world and runs contrary to our country's moral and philosophical foundation. The United States has always been, and must continue to be, a place that welcomes and embraces people of all religions and nationalities" (Alvarez 2019).

As part of the travel ban, Trump indefinitely banned the admission of refugees from the Syrian civil war and temporarily halted the U.S. Refugee Resettlement Program to ensure that refugees received adequate screening and did not pose a threat to national security. Opponents of these measures pointed out that refugees already underwent an intensive security screening process that took up to two years, and that none of the 800,000 refugees resettled in the United States since the terrorist attacks of September 11, 2001, had ever been involved in terrorist activity. They also claimed that terrorist groups would use these measures as evidence of U.S. government hostility toward Muslims to recruit new members.

In the fall of 2017, the Trump administration drastically reduced the annual cap on the number of refugees admitted into the United States to 45,000 for 2018, a record low and less than half the total allowed by President Barack Obama the previous year. The administration further reduced the cap to 30,000 for 2019 and to 18,000 for 2020, and it also announced plans to allow cities and states to refuse to accept refugees for resettlement. These moves came as the United Nations High Commissioner for Refugees reported that the number of refugees worldwide exceeded 20 million in 2018 (Narea 2019). Trump administration officials asserted that the reductions were necessary to allow U.S. Customs and Immigration Services (CIS) to focus on the large numbers of asylum seekers attempting to enter the country at the U.S.–Mexico border. "It would be irresponsible for the United States to go abroad seeking large numbers of refugees to resettle when the humanitarian and security crisis along the southern border already imposes an extraordinary burden on the U.S. immigration system," said a State Department official (Narea 2019).

Asylum is a form of protection granted by national governments to citizens of other nations who meet the definition of refugees under international law. Refugees are displaced persons who are unable or unwilling to return to their home countries due to a credible fear of persecution, torture, or violence "on account of race, religion, nationality, membership in a particular social group, or political opinion," according to the United Nations. People apply for asylum upon physically reaching the United States and then undergo a screening process to evaluate their claims of credible fear. Afterward, they receive either a removal order or a hearing before an immigration judge to determine whether they will be allowed to remain in the United States permanently. The asylum process is complex and often takes years to complete. Some asylum seekers remain in immigration detention facilities while their applications are processed, while others are released into the interior of the United States. On average, CIS granted around 23,700 asylum requests per year between 2007 and 2016 (American Immigration Council 2018).

Trump frequently expressed frustration with asylum laws, arguing that they provided incentives for Central American migrants to make the journey across Mexico to the U.S. border in hopes that the enormous backlog of asylum requests would enable them to remain in the United

States indefinitely. "The asylum procedures are ridiculous," he stated. "No place in the world has what we have in terms of ridiculous immigration laws" (Kullgren, Hesson, and Kumar 2019). In response, the Trump administration introduced several restrictions on asylum intended to stem the flow of Central American migrants. In January 2019, Trump implemented a new policy that required asylum seekers to remain in Mexico for the duration of their immigration proceedings. Critics charged that this policy forced traumatized and vulnerable refugees—many of them women and children—to wait in squalid, overcrowded camps in dangerous Mexican border towns.

A few months later, Trump announced another new policy that prohibited migrants from requesting asylum if they had resided in a safe third country before arriving in the United States. This policy aimed to prevent Central American migrants from trekking to the U.S. border and instead force them to seek asylum upon entering Mexico. Opponents called the policy unlawful and said they planned to challenge the policy in court. "This decision will cause a chain reaction—Central Americans who are fleeing for their lives being forced back into the burning house they are escaping," said immigrant rights advocate Pili Tobar. "A rational approach . . . is to treat this like the regional refugee crisis that it is and bolster our asylum and refugee process, instead of slamming the door shut with a childish hope that migrants will not come or conditions causing them to flee will get better on their own" (Kullgren, Hesson, and Kumar 2019).

Further Reading

Alvarez, Priscilla. 2019. "More Than 31,000 People Blocked from Entering U.S. by Trump Travel Ban." CNN, September 24, 2019. https://www.cnn.com /2019/09/24/politics/travel-ban-31000/index.html.

American Immigration Council. 2018. "Asylum in the United States." Fact Sheet, May 14, 2018. https://www.americanimmigrationcouncil.org/research /asylum-united-states.

Arce, Julissa. 2019. "Trump's Anti-Immigrant Rhetoric Was Never about Legality—It Was about Our Brown Skin." *Time*, August 6, 2019. https:// time.com/5645501/trump-anti-immigration-rhetoric-racism/.

Bier, David. 2017. "A Dozen Times Trump Has Equated His Travel Ban with a Muslim Ban." Cato Institute, August 14, 2017. https://www.cato.org/blog /dozen-times-trump-equated-travel-ban-muslim-ban.

Bump, Philip. 2019. "Migrants Targeted by ICE under Trump Are Much Less Likely to Have Criminal Records." SF Gate, July 19, 2019. https://www .sfgate.com/news/article/Migrants-targeted-by-ICE-under-Trump -are-much-14109373.php.

Flagg, Anna. 2018. "The Myth of the Criminal Immigrant." *New York Times*, March 30, 2018. https://www.nytimes.com/interactive/2018/03/30/upshot /crime-immigration-myth.html.

Fritze, John. 2019. "Trump Used Words Like 'Invasion' and 'Killer' to Discuss Immigrants at Rallies 500 Times: *USA TODAY* Analysis." *USA Today*, August 8, 2019. https://www.usatoday.com/story/news/politics/elections /2019/08/08/trump-immigrants-rhetoric-criticized-el-paso-dayton -shootings/1936742001/.

Haslett, Cheyenne. 2019. "Fact Check: Trump's Claims on Undocumented Immigrant Crime Rates." ABC News, January 16, 2019. https://abcnews .go.com/Politics/fact-check-trumps-claims-illegal-immigrant -crime-rates/story?id=60311860.

Krogstad, Jens Manuel, Jeffrey S. Passel, and D'Vera Cohn. 2019. "5 Facts about Illegal Immigration in the U.S." Pew Research Center, June 12, 2019. https://www.pewresearch.org/fact-tank/2019/06/12/5-facts-about -illegal-immigration-in-the-u-s/.

Kullgren, Ian, Ted Hesson, and Anita Kumar. 2019. "Trump Weighs Plan to Choke Off Asylum for Central Americans." *Politico*, May 30, 2019. https:// www.politico.com/story/2019/05/30/asylum-restrictions-trump -central-america-1489012.

Kwong, Jessica. 2019. "Donald Trump Says 'Chain Migration' Immigrants 'Are Not the People That We Want'—That Includes Melania's Parents." *Newsweek*, January 14, 2019. https://www.newsweek.com/donald-trump-chain -migration-immigrants-melania-1291210.

Narea, Nicole. 2019. "The U.S. Will Admit Just 18,000 Refugees in the Next Year." Vox, September 26, 2019. https://www.vox.com/policy-and-politics /2019/9/26/20886038/trump-refugee-cap-executive-order.

Phillips, Amber. 2017. "'They're Rapists.' President Trump's Campaign Launch Speech Two Years Later, Annotated." *Washington Post*, June 16, 2017. https://www.washingtonpost.com/news/the-fix/wp/2017/06/16/theyre -rapists-presidents-trump-campaign-launch-speech-two-years-later -annotated/.

Pierce, Sarah, Jessica Bolter, and Andrew Selee. 2018. "Trump's First Year on Immigration Policy: Rhetoric vs. Reality." Migration Policy Institute, January 2018. https://www.migrationpolicy.org/research/trump-first-year -immigration-policy-rhetoric-vs-reality.

Trump, Donald J. 2016. "Transcript of Donald Trump's Immigration Speech." *New York Times*, September 1, 2016. https://www.nytimes.com/2016/09 /02/us/politics/transcript-trump-immigration-speech.html.

Valverde, Miriam. 2019. "Donald Trump's Border Wall: How Much Has Been Built?" *PolitiFact*, August 30, 2019. https://www.politifact.com/truth-o-meter /article/2019/aug/30/donald-trumps-border-wall-how-much-has -really-been/.

The Flores Settlement Agreement (1997)

The basic conflict underlying the Trump administration's family separation policy stemmed from the Flores Settlement Agreement (FSA), which established legal standards for the treatment of unaccompanied alien children in U.S. government custody. The terms of the FSA required federal authorities to house minors in "safe and sanitary" facilities, give them access to basic necessities, and make "prompt and continuous" efforts to reunite them with family members. As interpreted by federal judges, the FSA also limited the amount of time minors could be kept in detention to 20 days, even when they crossed the border with their parents or other adult relatives. To comply with the FSA, previous administrations generally released all family members from immigration custody within 20 days and allowed them to remain in the United States while their asylum applications were processed.

Critics referred to this policy as "catch and release." They claimed that most people treated with such leniency never appeared for their asylum hearings and instead joined the large population of undocumented immigrants residing in the United States. Furthermore, they argued that the FSA encouraged parents—as well as unrelated adults, such as smugglers and human traffickers—to bring children across the border. "Aliens respond to incentives, and Flores remains a strong one," wrote Matthew Sussis of the Center for Immigration Studies. "If a Central American mother knows that bringing her child means that she can simply show up at a port of entry, claim credible fear [of persecution or violence], and then quickly be released from detention into the country regardless of the actual validity of her asylum claim, why wouldn't she do so?" (Sussis 2019).

Trump administration officials blamed the catch-and-release loophole for creating a humanitarian crisis at the border, as more and more migrant families and unaccompanied minors attempted to exploit the FSA to gain entry into the United States. In response, the Trump administration enacted a "zero tolerance" policy, which required U.S. Customs and Border Protection (CBP) officials to arrest and prosecute anyone caught crossing the border illegally, including migrants seeking asylum. With the FSA in place, however, the zero tolerance policy effectively forced immigration officials to separate migrant families that entered the United States together. When family separation ignited a firestorm of criticism, Trump and other administration officials blamed the FSA and insisted that they were only enforcing existing immigration laws.

The Flores Lawsuits

The FSA concluded a series of lawsuits that originated with the case of Jenny Lisette Flores, a 15-year-old girl from El Salvador. In 1985, Flores fled from her home country, which was then in the midst of a civil war characterized by deliberate attacks on civilians, and attempted to enter the United States. She was apprehended by agents with the U.S. Immigration and Naturalization Service (INS)—the agency that administered immigration laws and policies at that time—and sent to a detention center. Flores eventually hoped to join her mother, who had fled El Salvador after her husband was killed and found work in Los Angeles as the housekeeper for a well-known Hollywood actor. Her mother lacked documentation, however, and worried that the INS would deport her if she tried to claim her daughter. Although Flores had an aunt and cousin who had legal resident status in the United States and were willing to take custody of her, INS policy only permitted the release of unaccompanied minors to their legal guardians, rather than to "third-party adults," for the children's safety.

In the meantime, Flores was placed in a makeshift immigrant detention center in Pasadena, California. INS agents converted an old, two-story motel into a holding facility by erecting a barbed-wire fence around the perimeter, draining the swimming pool, and assigning men, women, and children to rooms. Flores and other minors in custody endured strip searches by guards and shared living quarters and bathrooms with unrelated adults of both sexes. Since the INS had no special accommodations for children, "the kids would essentially just hang around by the drained pool or on the balconies for days or weeks or months until it was determined what to do with them," recalled immigration attorney Carlos Holguín. "There were no standards whatsoever that the INS adhered to or that they were required to adhere to with respect to detention of minors" (NPR 2018).

Holguín and other attorneys associated with civil rights groups—including the American Civil Liberties Union (ACLU), the Center for Human Rights and Constitutional Law, and the National Center for Youth Law—filed a class-action lawsuit on behalf of detained migrant children, with Flores as the lead plaintiff. The lawsuit sought to establish standards for the treatment of unaccompanied migrant children held in custody by U.S. immigration authorities. It also challenged the INS policy that only allowed children to be released to parents or legal guardians. "The lawsuit basically argued two things," Holguín recalled. "One is that the INS should screen other available adults and release children to them if they appeared to be competent and, you know, not molesters and things of that nature, and secondly, that the government needed to improve the conditions existing in facilities in which it held minors to meet minimum child welfare standards" (NPR 2018).

The lawsuit wound its way through the federal court system for several years. It eventually became known as *Flores v. Reno* when Janet Reno, who served as U.S. attorney general under President Bill Clinton, became the defendant. In 1988, a district court judge in California ruled in favor of the plaintiffs, declaring strip searches of minor detainees unconstitutional and ordering the INS to release migrant children to responsible adults other than their legal guardians. Although a three-judge panel of the Ninth Circuit Court of Appeals overturned the district court decision in 1990, the full court disagreed and voted 7–4 to uphold the earlier ruling for the plaintiffs. In 1992, the case reached the U.S. Supreme Court, which reversed the lower court decisions and ruled 7–2 in favor of the INS. Writing for the majority, Justice Antonin Scalia asserted that immigration officials had the constitutional authority to detain migrant children and to decline to release them to third parties. "Where a juvenile has no available parent, close relative, or legal guardian, where the government does not intend to punish the child, and where the conditions of governmental custody are decent and humane, such custody surely does not violate the Constitution," the opinion stated (U.S. Supreme Court 1993).

Justice John Paul Stevens penned a dissent, which Justice Harry Blackmun joined. Stevens argued that the federal government failed to demonstrate a compelling interest in detaining migrant children indefinitely rather than releasing them to the care of responsible adults. "This case involves the institutional detention of juveniles who pose no risk of flight and no threat of harm to themselves or to others. They are children who have responsible third parties available to receive and care for them; many, perhaps most, of them will never be deported," he wrote. "In my view, an agency's interest in minimizing administrative costs is a patently inadequate justification for the detention of harmless children, even when the conditions of detention are 'good enough'" (U.S. Supreme Court 1993).

After the Supreme Court ruled in its favor, the INS continued detaining unaccompanied migrant children, while immigrant rights advocates continued visiting detention facilities and raising concerns about the conditions in which the children were held. Immigration attorneys filed several additional lawsuits intended to pressure the INS to protect the rights of children in its custody. In 1997, the nonprofit organization Human Rights Watch—which investigates and publicizes human rights abuses by governments around the world—released a report criticizing the INS's handling of child migrant detention. *Slipping through the Cracks: Unaccompanied Children Detained by the U.S. Immigration and Naturalization Service* charged that conditions at INS detention facilities in Arizona and California "violate the children's rights under international law, the U.S. Constitution, U.S. statutory provisions, INS regulations, and the terms of court orders binding on the INS" (Human Rights Watch 1997).

Human Rights Watch investigators expressed concern about migrant children and teenagers being held in prison-like conditions for extended periods of time. They noted that most of the detainees did not speak English and lacked awareness of their legal rights, leaving them unable to advocate for themselves and vulnerable to exploitation. "Children in INS detention are invisible: they have slipped through the cracks in America's legal system," the report stated. "They are arrested by the INS, detained in highly restrictive settings, and provided with little information about their legal rights and status. . . . Many [of] them remain in detention for months on end, bewildered and frightened, denied meaningful access to attorneys and to their relatives" (Human Rights Watch 1997). The organization recommended that Congress pass legislation to place unaccompanied migrant children in the custody of child welfare agencies to eliminate the conflict of interest between the INS's enforcement and caregiving functions.

Doris Meissner, who served as INS commissioner in the Clinton administration, attempted to resolve the situation by signing the FSA. Under the FSA, the INS agreed to establish standards for the treatment of migrant children, which would include placing them in "the least restrictive setting appropriate to the child's age and special needs" and releasing them "without unnecessary delay" to legal guardians or other responsible adults (Gruwell 2018). The FSA also required immigration officials to provide detained minors with basic necessities to keep them safe and comfortable, including food, water, adult supervision, and access to medical care. Since the Supreme Court had already weighed in on INS detention policies, critics charged that Meissner gave in to pressure from pro-immigration activists by signing the FSA. They argued that the agreement loosened asylum restrictions and hampered the federal government's ability to enforce immigration laws.

Further Developments

In 2002, Congress shifted responsibility for enforcement of the nation's immigration laws to the newly created Department of Homeland

Security (DHS). The INS ceased to exist, and its functions transferred to three successor agencies—U.S. Citizenship and Immigration Services, U.S. Customs and Border Protection, and U.S. Immigration and Customs Enforcement—under the jurisdiction of the DHS. In 2008, Congress passed the William Wilberforce Trafficking Victims Protection Reauthorization Act, which included provisions intended to protect the rights of unaccompanied migrant children. It required immigration enforcement agencies to transfer custody of minors to the Office of Refugee Resettlement—an agency within the Department of Health and Human Services charged with safeguarding the interests of people granted asylum in the United States—within 72 hours if they could not be placed with relatives.

In 2015, in response to an increase in the number of migrant families from Central America crossing the U.S. border, the Obama administration asked a federal court to modify the FSA to allow immigration agencies to detain children with their parents while their asylum applications were processed. District Court Judge Dolly Gee denied the request. In doing so, she ruled that the FSA requirements applied to children who entered the United States as part of family units as well as to unaccompanied minors. She also interpreted the FSA's stipulation that the government must release children from detention "without unnecessary delay" to mean 20 days. In effect, the ruling forced immigration authorities to release entire migrant families within 20 days to remain in compliance with the FSA, establishing what critics called the catch-and-release policy.

In 2016, the Ninth Circuit Court of Appeals affirmed that the FSA applied to all children in immigration custody, but it also held that the FSA did not require the government to release accompanying adult family members. "This ruling laid the groundwork for the current crisis at the border," according to Sussis, "in which children are released while their parents can still be detained awaiting hearings—hence, the 'separation' of families" (Sussis 2019). Critics claimed that the ruling encouraged migrant families to cross the border and initiate the asylum process in hopes of being released into the United States while their applications were being processed. In 2018, CBP apprehended nearly 93,000 people seeking asylum from a credible fear of persecution or violence in their home countries—a figure ten times higher than a decade earlier (Sussis 2019). Immigrant rights activists, on the other hand, attributed the rise in asylum seekers to an increase in poverty, gang violence, political chaos, environmental impacts of climate change, and other problems in Mexico and Central America.

Some critics called on Congress to pass legislation to supersede the FSA, while others argued that DHS had the authority to develop new federal regulations for the treatment of migrant children. In the meantime, immigrant rights advocates continued to demand FSA protections for detained migrant children. "I am completely surprised, even to this day, that [the FSA] continues to be the main bulwark against the government running roughshod over the rights of these children," Holguín acknowledged. "Had anyone ever [said], especially in 1985, that this battle is going to continue on, that the work you are doing now is going to have some impact for the benefit of children in 2019, I never would have predicted that" (Barrera 2019).

Further Reading

Barrera, Jorge. 2019. "How a 35-Year-Old Case of a Migrant Girl from El Salvador Still Fuels the Border Debate." CBC Radio, June 28, 2019. https://www .cbc.ca/radio/day6/detained-migrant-children-resident-orcas-stranger -things-stonewall-at-50-and-more-1.5192640/how-a-35-year-old-case-of -a-migrant-girl-from-el-salvador-still-fuels-the-border-debate-1.5192662.

Elkin, Elizabeth, and Emily Smith. 2018. "What Is the Flores Settlement?" CNN, July 10, 2018. https://www.cnn.com/2018/07/10/politics/flores-settlement -history/index.html.

Gruwell, Abbie. 2018. "Unaccompanied Minors and the Flores Settlement Agreement: What to Know." National Council of State Legislatures, October 30, 2018. http://www.ncsl.org/blog/2018/10/30/unaccompanied-minors -and-the-flores-settlement-agreement-what-to-know.aspx.

Human Rights Watch. 1997. *Slipping through the Cracks: Unaccompanied Children Detained by the U.S. Immigration and Naturalization Service.* New York: Human Rights Watch Children's Project, April 1997. https://www.hrw .org/sites/default/files/reports/us974.pdf.

NPR. 2018. "The History of the Flores Settlement and Its Effects on Immigration." Capital Public Radio, June 22, 2018. http://www.capradio.org/news /npr/story?storyid=622678753.

Sussis, Matthew. 2019. "The History of the Flores Settlement." Center for Immigration Studies, February 11, 2019. https://cis.org/Report/History-Flores -Settlement.

U.S. Supreme Court. 1993. *Reno v. Flores,* 507 U.S. 292, March 23, 1993. FindLaw. https://caselaw.findlaw.com/us-supreme-court/507/292.html.

White House. 2019. "President Donald J. Trump Is Taking Action to Close the Loopholes That Fuel the Humanitarian Crisis on Our Border." Fact Sheet, August 21, 2019. https://www.whitehouse.gov/briefings-statements/president -donald-j-trump-taking-action-close-loopholes-fuel-humanitarian-crisis -border/.

Trump Enacts the Zero Tolerance Policy (2018)

Of the many changes to U.S. immigration policy made by President Donald Trump, the "zero tolerance policy" he enacted in May 2018 ranks among the most controversial. This policy required U.S. Customs and Border Protection (CBP) officials to arrest and prosecute anyone caught crossing the border without authorization. Although entering the country without the approval of an immigration officer was always a misdemeanor offense, many people apprehended at the border had avoided criminal prosecution prior to this time. Some returned to their countries of origin voluntarily, while others went through civil deportation proceedings. In addition, previous administrations often made exceptions for first-time offenders, families with children, and people seeking asylum based on a credible fear of violence in their home countries.

Federal laws and court rulings made the situation particularly complicated when children crossed the border illegally, whether unaccompanied or as part of family units. The 1997 Flores Settlement Agreement (FSA), as interpreted by federal judges, limited the amount of time minors could be kept in immigration detention facilities to 20 days. To comply with the FSA, previous administrations generally released all family members from immigration custody within 20 days and allowed them to remain in the United States while awaiting their asylum or removal hearings—which could take years. Detractors referred to this policy as "catch and release" and claimed that it created an incentive for migrant families and unaccompanied minors to enter the United States illegally. Trump vowed to eliminate the catch-and-release loophole, which he blamed for causing a humanitarian crisis at the border.

The zero tolerance policy effectively forced immigration officials to separate migrant families that entered the United States together. When adult family members were arrested and prosecuted, their children became unaccompanied minors subject to the FSA restrictions on child detention. The zero tolerance policy thus became known as the family separation policy, as it resulted in more than 2,000 migrant children being taken away from their adult caregivers over a six-week period. "If you cross the border unlawfully, even a first offense, we're going to prosecute you," warned Attorney General Jeff Sessions. "If you're smuggling a child, we're going to prosecute you, and that child will be separated from you, probably, as required by law. If you don't want your child to be separated, then don't bring them across the border illegally" (Kopan 2018a).

Policy Shift Separates Migrant Families

The idea of prosecuting all illegal border crossers as an enforcement tool and deterrent measure did not originate with the Trump administration. President George W. Bush enacted a limited version of the zero tolerance policy in 2005 with his Operation Streamline program. Beginning with one small section of border in Texas, the Bush administration prosecuted all unlawful entrants in expedited, assembly-line trials. President Barack Obama also stepped up prosecutions of people apprehended at the border as a way of dealing with a migration crisis, although his administration often made exceptions for first-time offenders, asylum seekers, and families with children.

From the time Trump took office in 2017, immigration hardliners in his administration considered reviving Operation Streamline and expanding it to cover more sections of the southern border. They also discussed administrative means of discouraging migrant families and unaccompanied minors from attempting to enter the United States. In April 2017, for instance, Sessions instructed the U.S. Immigration and Customs Enforcement Agency (ICE) to target parents and other adult sponsors for arrest and prosecution when they arrived to claim unaccompanied minors from immigration custody. White House policy adviser Stephen Miller, Trump chief of staff John Kelly, and other officials also tried to convince Congress to amend the FSA to eliminate the catch-and-release loophole in exchange for restoring legal protection to Deferred Action for Childhood Arrivals (DACA) recipients.

During Trump's first months in office, his repeated vows to increase border security and enforcement contributed to a decrease in migrants attempting to cross the U.S.–Mexico border. From January through August 2017, CBP reported a 50 percent reduction in apprehensions from the same period a year earlier. Even as the overall number of unlawful entrants fell, however, the number of families and unaccompanied minors continued to rise. From April through December 2017, average monthly apprehensions of migrant families increased from 1,000 to 8,000, while monthly apprehensions of unaccompanied minors grew from 1,000 to 4,000 (Pierce, Bolter, and Selee 2018). Frustrated by these figures, administration officials claimed that the continued influx of families and children meant an increasing number of people were exploiting the catch-and-release loophole.

Immigrant rights advocates, on the other hand, attributed the growth in family migration to other factors, especially socioeconomic conditions in the Northern Triangle countries of Central America (El Salvador, Guatemala, and Honduras). They pointed out that El Salvador and Honduras had the highest homicide rates in the world in 2016. The infamous MS-13 street gang, with 60,000 members in Central America, was largely responsible for the violence, as they used intimidation and murder to recruit new members among poor and at-risk youth. Many Central American young people and families also migrated in search of economic opportunities. In both Guatemala and Honduras, an estimated 60 percent of citizens lived in poverty, with the situation growing worse each year through the effects of climate change on agricultural production. These factors contributed to an increase in asylum applicants citing a credible fear of returning to the Northern Triangle countries from around 14,000 in 2012 to more than 99,000 in 2018 (BBC News 2019).

In the spring of 2018, the Trump administration announced its intention to arrest and prosecute anyone caught crossing the border without authorization, regardless of whether they were seeking asylum or traveling with children. "Congress has failed to pass effective legislation that serves the national interest—that closes dangerous loopholes and fully funds a wall along our southern border," Sessions said in introducing the policy on May 7. "As a result, a crisis has erupted at our Southwest Border that necessitates an escalated effort to prosecute those who choose to illegally cross our border" (Arthur 2018). Immediately after the zero tolerance policy took effect, some administration officials acknowledged that it would lead to the separation of migrant families. "A big name of the game is deterrence," Kelly stated. "The children will be taken care of—put into foster care or whatever—but the big point is they elected to come illegally into the United States, and this is a technique that no one hopes will be used extensively or for very long" (Davis and Shear 2018).

Within a few weeks, reports began to trickle out of detention facilities indicating that immigration authorities were taking migrant children away from their parents. On June 14, for instance, CNN related the story of a Honduran mother who said federal officials snatched her infant daughter from her arms as she breastfed her in a Texas detention center. Although administration officials initially denied separating families, the following day a Department of Homeland Security (DHS) spokesperson admitted that the zero tolerance policy had resulted in 1,995 children being separated from 1,940 "alleged adult guardians" between April 19 and May 31 (Kopan 2018b).

Family Separation Creates Uproar and Confusion

As the effects of the zero tolerance policy became clear, the Trump administration came under intense criticism. Scenes of CBP officers taking tearful children from their parents' arms, along with reports of traumatized children being held in crowded and unsanitary conditions, generated public outrage and widespread protests. Opponents derided the separation of families as inhumane and a violation of human rights. Former First Lady Laura Bush published an opinion piece in the *Washington Post* comparing the family separation policy to the internment of Japanese Americans during World War II. "This zero-tolerance policy is cruel. It is immoral. And it breaks my heart," she wrote. Senator John McCain (R-AZ) called on Trump to rescind the family separation policy immediately, calling it "an affront to the decency of the American people, and contrary to principles and values upon which our nation was founded." Representative Will Hurd (R-TX) asserted that "taking kids from their mothers is not preventing terrorists or drugs from coming into this country. And so why we would even think that this is a tool that is needed to defend our borders is insane to me" (Chappell and Taylor 2018).

Representative Beto O'Rourke (D-TX) organized a Father's Day protest march outside a detention facility holding migrant children in Tornillo, Texas. The Families Belong Together Coalition organized more than 600 local rallies in all 50 states. Prominent religious leaders also voiced objections to the zero tolerance policy, including Pope Francis and the U.S. Conference of Catholic Bishops. "It's disgraceful and it's terrible to see families ripped apart, and I don't support that one bit," said evangelist Franklin Graham, an outspoken Trump supporter (Chappell and Taylor 2018). Sessions responded to the criticism by invoking the Bible to reinforce his contention that migrant families could avoid separation by respecting U.S. immigration laws. "I would cite you to the Apostle Paul and his clear and wise command in Romans 13 to obey the laws of the government," he said. "Because God has ordained them for the purpose of order" (Davis and Shear 2018).

As controversy swirled around the family separation policy, Trump administration officials made contradictory and false statements in attempting to justify and defend it. DHS Secretary Kirstjen Nielsen, for instance, initially claimed that immigration officials only separated migrant families if they doubted the parental relationship or felt concern for the children's safety. Later, she acknowledged that family separations occurred regularly but attributed the problem to laws put in place by previous administrations. "We do not have a policy of separating families at the border. Period," Nielsen stated. "What has changed is that we no longer exempt entire classes of people who break the law. Everyone is subject to prosecution" (Rizzo 2018). She pointed out that U.S. citizens who violated the law were also separated from their children upon being arrested.

Some critics accused the Trump administration of using migrant children as a political tool to pressure Congress to reform immigration laws. "We do not want to separate children from their parents, you can be sure of that," Sessions stated. "If we build the wall, we pass some legislation, we close some loopholes, we won't face these terrible choices" (Chappell and Taylor 2018). Trump falsely claimed that the Obama administration was responsible for the family separation policy and insisted that he was powerless to end the crisis. "I hate the children being taken away," he said. "The Democrats have to change their law. That's their law" (McArdle 2018). Republicans controlled both houses of Congress at that time, however, and refused to consider immigration bills that did not include funding for Trump's border wall. Even some Republicans demanded that the president revoke the zero tolerance policy. "I think the White House can fix it if they want to," said Senator Orrin Hatch (R-UT). "The way it's being handled right now isn't acceptable. I think we've got to try and keep families together and do whatever it takes to keep them together" (Chappell and Taylor 2018).

On June 18, 2018, CNN published the results of a nationwide poll showing that two-thirds of Americans disapproved of the family separation policy. In addition, Trump's public approval ratings on immigration dropped to an all-time low of 35 percent (Sparks 2018). In the face of mounting public outrage and political pressure, Trump signed Executive Order 13841 rescinding the zero tolerance policy on June 20, 2018. Entitled "Affording Congress an Opportunity to Address Family Separation," the order emphasized the administration's commitment to rigorous enforcement of laws prohibiting illegal immigration. It also outlined a goal of maintaining family unity by detaining parents and children together, expanding the number of immigration facilities capable of housing families, and prioritizing the legal resolution of asylum applications and removal hearings involving families. "We're going to have strong—very strong borders, but we're going to keep the families together," Trump explained. "I didn't like the sight or the feeling of families being separated" (Gonzales 2018).

Immigration hardliners accused Trump of capitulating to his political opponents by signing the order. Immigrant rights advocates also criticized the measure, arguing that it did not do enough to reunite the migrant families that had been harmed by the policy or to protect them moving forward. "First, there are more than 2,000 children already separated from their parents; the executive order does nothing to address that nightmare," said Michelle Brané of the Women's Refugee Commission. "Second, this executive order effectively creates family prisons, which we already know are a threat to the well-being of children" (Gonzales 2018).

As part of the executive order, Trump instructed the Department of Justice to file a new legal challenge to the FSA. The administration sought to modify the agreement to allow immigration agencies to hold migrant children with their parents in family detention centers for periods longer than 20 days. Judge Dolly Gee denied the request, calling it "a cynical attempt . . . to shift responsibility to the judiciary for over 20 years of congressional inaction and ill-considered executive action that have led to the current stalemate" (Arthur 2018). Trump administration officials expressed frustration with the ruling, claiming that it forced immigration agencies to either resume the catch-and-release policy for migrant families or continue separating families to comply with the FSA restrictions on child detention.

Further Reading

Arthur, Andrew R. 2018. "Judge Dolly Gee Issues a New Flores Order." Center for Immigration Studies, July 12, 2018. https://cis.org/Arthur/Judge-Dolly -Gee-Issues-New-Flores-Order.

BBC News. 2019. "Migrant Children in the U.S.: The Bigger Picture Explained." July 2, 2019. https://www.bbc.com/news/world-us-canada-44532437.

Chappell, Bill, and Jessica Taylor. 2018. "Defiant Homeland Security Secretary Defends Family Separations." NPR, June 18, 2018. https://www.npr.org /2018/06/18/620972542/we-do-not-have-a-policy-of-separating-families -dhs-secretary-nielsen-says.

Davis, Julie Hirschfeld, and Michael D. Shear. 2018. "How Trump Came to Enforce a Practice of Separating Migrant Families." *New York Times*, June 16, 2018. https://www.nytimes.com/2018/06/16/us/politics/family -separation-trump.html.

Gonzales, Richard. 2018. "Trump's Executive Order on Family Separation: What It Does and Doesn't Do." NPR, June 20, 2018. https://www.npr.org/2018 /06/20/622095441/trump-executive-order-on-family-separation-what-it -does-and-doesnt-do.

Kopan, Tal. 2018a. "New DHS Policy Could Separate Families Caught Crossing the Border Illegally." CNN, May 7, 2018. https://www.cnn.com/2018/05 /07/politics/illegal-immigration-border-prosecutions-families-separated /index.html.

Kopan, Tal. 2018b. "DHS: 2,000 Children Separated from Parents at Border." CNN, June 16, 2018. https://www.cnn.com/2018/06/15/politics/dhs-family -separation-numbers/index.html.

McArdle, Mairead. 2018. "White House Blames Democrats for Separation of Families at Border." *National Review*, June 15, 2018. https://www.national review.com/news/white-house-blames-democrats-for-separation-of -families-at-border/.

Pierce, Sarah, Jessica Bolter, and Andrew Selee. 2018. "Trump's First Year on Immigration Policy: Rhetoric vs. Reality." Migration Policy Institute, January 2018. https://www.migrationpolicy.org/research/trump-first-year -immigration-policy-rhetoric-vs-reality.

Rizzo, Salvador. 2018. "The Facts about Trump's Policy of Separating Families at the Border." *Washington Post*, June 19, 2018. https://www.washingtonpost .com/news/fact-checker/wp/2018/06/19/the-facts-about-trumps-policy -of-separating-families-at-the-border/.

Sparks, Grace. 2018. "Majority Oppose Policy That Causes Family Separation, but Republicans Approve." CNN, June 18, 2018. https://www.cnn.com /2018/06/18/politics/immigration-trump-approval/index.html.

Ms. L v. ICE Requires Family Reunification (2018)

When President Donald Trump signed Executive Order 13841 on June 20, 2018, revoking his unpopular zero tolerance policy, many Americans hoped that it marked the end of the migrant family separation crisis at the southern border. Less than a week later, on June 26, a federal judge issued an injunction in the class-action lawsuit *Ms. L v. U.S. Customs and Immigration Enforcement (ICE)* requiring immigration officials to reunite 2,648 migrant children with the adult caregivers from whom they had been separated while the policy remained in place.

Over the next several months, however, federal agencies struggled to identify, locate, and reconnect the members of migrant families. While adults accused of immigration violations remained in the custody of ICE—a division of the U.S. Department of Homeland Security (DHS)— migrant children (whether unaccompanied or separated from adult caregivers) were transferred to the Office of Refugee Resettlement (ORR) within the U.S. Department of Health and Human Services (HHS). These agencies did not maintain a central database of migrants in custody or establish a process to help reunite families detained separately. Instead, officials merely posted a toll-free number for migrant parents to call for information. "There is no tracking system," said Anthony Enriquez, director of Catholic Charities' Unaccompanied Refugee Minors Program. "No comprehensive information-sharing system, and no reliable method by which we can have real-time data on the actual location of a parent so that family members can be brought back together" (Goldberg 2019).

During the family reunification process, new information came to light indicating that the Trump administration had begun separating migrant families well before the zero tolerance policy took effect in May 2018. Critics noted that family separation thus may have affected thousands more people than the Trump administration admitted, yet poor record-keeping made it difficult to determine the exact numbers. "It may be tempting to think that Donald Trump's 'zero tolerance' policy, which led to the separation of many migrant families, is a tragedy from our recent past," wrote Steve Benen of MSNBC. "The president and his team implemented a cruel approach; there was a public backlash; the White House scaled back its policy; and a federal court ordered an end to the brutal fiasco. The problem—one of them, anyway—is that the tragedy is *ongoing*" (Benen 2019).

A Federal Judge Halts Family Separation

Attorneys with the American Civil Liberties Union (ACLU) filed a lawsuit challenging the separation of migrant parents and children in February 2018, several months before the Trump administration publicly announced its zero tolerance policy. The original case concerned a woman from the Democratic Republic of the Congo, referred to in court documents as Ms. L, and her seven-year-old daughter, known as S.S. Ms. L fled from ethnic conflict and pervasive sexual violence against women in her home country. She arrived at a port of entry on the U.S.–Mexico border in November 2017 and requested asylum in the United States. Following a preliminary interview, an immigration officer found that Ms. L demonstrated a credible fear of persecution or violence if she returned to her country of origin. Ms. L and S.S. then entered an immigration detention center in San Diego, California to await processing of their asylum application.

Less than a week later, immigration officials forcibly took S.S. away from her mother. "When the officers separated them, Ms. L could hear her daughter in the next room frantically screaming that she wanted to remain with her mother," according to the ACLU lawsuit. "No one explained to Ms. L why they were taking her daughter away from her or where her daughter was going or even when she would next see her daughter" (Hayoun 2018). While Ms. L remained in ICE custody in San Diego, S.S. was transferred to an ORR facility for unaccompanied minor refugees in Chicago, Illinois—more than 2,000 miles away. Mother and daughter remained apart, unable to communicate with each other, and deeply traumatized for four months, until immigration authorities released Ms. L from detention in March 2018, shortly after the ACLU filed its lawsuit.

In *Ms. L v. ICE*, the ACLU argued that separating migrant parents from their minor children served no legitimate government interest, infringed on the rights of asylum seekers, and violated the due process clause of the Fourteenth Amendment to the Constitution. Although the initial lawsuit sought to reunite Ms. L with her daughter, ACLU attorneys soon expanded it to a class action representing all migrant parents who were separated from their minor children through the Trump administration's immigration policies. "According to advocates, there have been hundreds of separations nationwide," said Lee Gelernt of the ACLU's National Immigrants' Rights Project. "Based on reports, the administration apparently believes that separating young kids from their parents will deter future asylum applicants" (Hayoun 2018).

A spokesman for the DHS denied that the Trump administration systematically separated migrant families. "DHS does not currently have a policy of separating women and children. However, we retain the authority to do so in certain circumstances—particularly to protect a child from potential smuggling and trafficking activities," the official said. "We ask that members of the public and media view advocacy group claims that we are separating women and children for reasons other than to protect the child with the level of skepticism they deserve" (Kennedy 2018). In the case of Ms. L, the ACLU lawsuit noted that immigration officials never raised any concerns regarding her fitness as a parent or her daughter's safety. "Whether or not the Trump administration wants to call this a 'policy,' it certainly is engaged in a widespread practice of tearing children away from their parents," Gelernt stated (Kennedy 2018).

On May 7, 2018, the Trump administration formally announced its zero tolerance policy, which required immigration officials to arrest and prosecute anyone caught crossing the border illegally, even asylum seekers and parents traveling with children. This policy effectively forced immigration authorities to separate minor children from adult caregivers due to laws and court rulings limiting the amount of time migrant children could spend in detention to 20 days. It resulted in more than 2,000 children being taken away from their parents before Trump rescinded it on June 20 in the face of widespread criticism and protests.

On June 26, U.S. District Judge Dana Sabraw issued a ruling in the ACLU's class-action lawsuit, which he expanded to cover all the migrant parents and children who had been separated during enforcement of the zero tolerance policy. Sabraw ordered immigration authorities to take affirmative action to reunite children younger than five with their parents within 14 days and to reunite all other migrant families within 30 days. Finally, the judge declared that no further family separations should occur "unless there is a determination that the parent is unfit or presents a danger to the child" (Jarrett 2018).

While Sabraw acknowledged the government's authority to enact the zero tolerance policy, he sharply criticized the administration for failing to protect the rights and interests of the migrant families affected by it. "The facts set forth before the court portray reactive governance—responses to address a chaotic circumstance of the government's own making," the judge wrote. "The government readily keeps track of personal property of detainees in criminal and immigration proceedings. Money, important documents, and automobiles, to name a few, are routinely catalogued, stored, tracked, and produced upon a detainee's release, at all levels—state and federal, citizen and alien. Yet, the government has no system in place to keep track of, provide effective communication with, and promptly produce alien children. The unfortunate reality is that under the present system migrant children are not accounted for with the same efficiency and accuracy as property. Certainly, that cannot satisfy the requirements of due process" (Jarrett 2018).

Family Reunification Proceeds Slowly

Sabraw ordered the Trump administration to report on its progress toward meeting his deadlines for reunifying migrant families. By the time 30 days expired on July 26, the government had reunited more than 1,000 children affected by the zero tolerance policy with their parents or other adult relatives. More than 900 children had not yet rejoined their families, however, and in around half of those cases, the parents had been deported to their countries of origin, while the children remained in the United States. "It's the reality of a policy that was in place that resulted in large numbers of families being separated without forethought as to reunification and keeping track of people," the judge said (Yan 2018).

As federal agencies worked to reunite the migrant families that had been separated during the six-week period when the zero tolerance policy was in effect, evidence came to light suggesting that the Trump administration had begun separating parents from children almost a year earlier. An internal investigation by the HHS Office of the Inspector General revealed that immigration officials secretly launched a pilot program for the zero tolerance policy in July 2017 by bringing criminal charges against everyone who crossed a small stretch of border near El Paso, Texas. By August 2017, the percentage of migrant children transferred to ORR after being separated from a parent increased to 3.6 percent, up from 0.3 percent in 2016, when separations only occurred out of concern for the child's safety (Small 2019). Over the next few months, immigrant rights advocates received numerous complaints from people like Ms. L, who were separated from their children after seeking asylum in the United States. The Trump administration did not publicly acknowledge separating migrant families until May 2018, however, when Sessions announced the zero tolerance policy.

By December 2018, the HHS inspector general increased the number of children who were separated from their parents and subject to reunification to 2,737. In March 2019, Judge Sabraw granted the ACLU's request to expand the class covered in the lawsuit to include all the migrant families separated between July 1, 2017, and June 25, 2018. The court order requiring the federal government to reunite migrant families thus could apply to hundreds or thousands of additional parents and children. Due to poor planning, communication, and record-keeping by federal agencies, however, immigration officials could not determine the exact number of children who remained separated from their parents. "When there is an allegation of wrong on this scale, one of the most fundamental obligations of the law is to bring to light what that wrong was and what is the scope of the wrong," Sabraw said in his ruling. "What are the numbers, who are they, where are they?" (Small 2019).

The Trump administration contested the ruling. Jallyn Sualog, deputy director of the ORR, argued that her agency lacked the time and resources to manually review case files for the 47,000 migrant children who came into U.S. immigration custody from July 2017 through June 2018 to determine which ones had crossed the border unaccompanied and which had been separated from parents or legal guardians. Sualog said that identifying and reuniting all the separated families could take two years and might not be "within the realm of the possible." She also asserted that it might be preferable to leave migrant children with foster families or sponsors, because reuniting them with parents "could interfere with the child's routine and currently established relationships" (Benen 2019).

Sabraw rejected the administration's reasoning and insisted that immigration officials had a responsibility to account for all the migrant children who had been separated from their parents. "Although the process for identifying newly proposed class members may be burdensome, it clearly can be done," the judge wrote. "The hallmark of a civilized society is measured by how it treats its people and those within its borders" (Small 2019). He gave the Trump administration six months to determine a final figure. In October 2019, the Justice Department disclosed that an additional 1,556 migrant children—the majority of whom were age 12 or under, and more than 200 of whom were under age 5—had been separated from their parents during the time period specified in the ACLU lawsuit (Sacchetti 2019). Democrats in Congress vowed to hold the administration accountable for reuniting the migrant families. "This is government-sanctioned child abuse," said U.S. Representative Rosa DeLauro (D-CT), "and the whole ordeal is a stain on our nation and our values" (Flaherty 2019).

Further Reading

ACLU. 2019. "Ms. L v. ICE: Status Report." September 11, 2019. https://www
.aclu.org/legal-document/ms-l-v-ice-status-report-9-11-19.
Benen, Steve. 2019. "Trump Admin: Reuniting Migrant Families May Not Be
Possible." MSNBC, February 5, 2019. http://www.msnbc.com/rachel
-maddow-show/trump-admin-reuniting-migrant-families-may-not-be
-possible.
Flaherty, Anne. 2019. "Under President Donald Trump's Administration, More
Kids Separated at Border than Originally Estimated." ABC News, January
18, 2019. https://abcnews.go.com/Politics/president-donald-trumps-admin
istration-kids-separated-border-originally/story?id=60447930.
Gerstein, Josh, and Ted Hesson. 2018. "Federal Judge Orders Trump Administration to Reunite Migrant Families." *Politico*, June 26, 2018. https://www
.politico.com/story/2018/06/26/judge-orders-trump-reunite-migrant
-families-678809.
Goldberg, Michelle. 2019. "The Terrible Things Trump Is Doing in Our Name."
New York Times, June 21, 2019. https://www.nytimes.com/2019/06/21
/opinion/family-separation-trump-migrants.html.
Gonzales, Richard. 2018. "Trump's Executive Order on Family Separation: What
It Does and Doesn't Do." NPR, June 20, 2018. https://www.npr.org/2018
/06/20/622095441/trump-executive-order-on-family-separation-what-it
-does-and-doesnt-do.
Hayoun, Massoud. 2018. "The Trump Administration Is Reportedly Separating
Hundreds of Immigrant Children from Their Parents." *Pacific Standard*,
February 28, 2018. https://psmag.com/social-justice/the-trump-admin
istration-is-reportedly-separating-hundreds-of-immigrant-children-from
-their-parents.
Jarrett, Laura. 2018. "Federal Judge Orders Reunification of Parents and Children, End to Most Family Separations at Border." CNN, June 27, 2018.
https://www.cnn.com/2018/06/26/politics/federal-court-order-family
-separations/index.html.
Kennedy, Merrit. 2018. "ACLU Sues ICE for Allegedly Separating 'Hundreds' of
Migrant Families." NPR, March 9, 2018. https://www.npr.org/sections
/thetwo-way/2018/03/09/592374637/aclu-sues-ice-for-allegedly
-separating-hundreds-of-migrant-families.
Sacchetti, Maria. 2019. "ACLU Says 1,500 More Migrant Children Were Taken
from Parents by the Trump Administration." *Washington Post*, October 24,
2019. https://www.washingtonpost.com/immigration/aclu-says-1500-more

-migrant-children-were-taken-from-parents-by-trump-administration
/2019/10/24/d014f818-f6aa-11e9-a285-882a8e386a96_story.html.

Small, Julie. 2019. "Judge: Immigration Must Account for Thousands More Migrant Kids Split Up from Parents." NPR, March 19, 2019. https://www .npr.org/2019/03/09/701935587/judge-immigration-must-identify -thousands-more-migrant-kids-separated-from-paren.

Yan, Holly. 2018. "The US Must Reunite Separated Families by Today—But over 900 Probably Won't Be Reunited." CNN, July 26, 2018. https://www.cnn .com/2018/07/25/politics/separated-families-by-the-numbers/index .html.

Immigration Issues Dominate the 2018 Midterm Election (2018)

During his 2016 presidential campaign, Republican Donald Trump frequently portrayed immigration as a threat to Americans' national security, public safety, economic advancement, and cultural unity. His hardline stance on immigration resonated with conservative voters and helped him win the election. During his first 18 months in office, Trump backed up his campaign promises by enacting a number of strict new immigration policies, such as banning travel by citizens of predominantly Muslim countries, revoking protected status for Deferred Action for Childhood Arrivals (DACA) program recipients, ordering high-profile raids by U.S. Immigration and Customs Enforcement (ICE) agents, and separating migrant children from their parents at the U.S.–Mexico border. Although these measures generated considerable controversy, they also helped cement Trump's reputation with his political base.

As the November 2018 midterm election approached, many observers characterized it as a referendum on Trump's presidency. Republicans controlled both chambers of Congress for the first two years of Trump's term. Democrats needed a net gain of 2 seats to achieve a majority in the Senate—where Republican incumbents only had to defend 9 of the 35 seats being contested—and a net gain of 23 seats among the 435 being contested to win a majority in the House of Representatives. Given the increasing polarization of the electorate, some analysts predicted that whichever party proved more effective in getting its voters to the polls would control Congress, giving it the ability to advance—or thwart— Trump's legislative agenda.

In the weeks leading up to the election, Trump returned to immigration as the primary focus of his speeches, campaign rallies, press conferences, and social media posts in an effort to energize his base and motivate his supporters to vote. Specifically, Trump repeatedly warned about a "migrant caravan" full of violent criminals from Central America threatening to invade the United States. "Every time you see a Caravan," he tweeted, "or people illegally coming, or attempting to come, into our Country illegally, think of and blame the Democrats for not giving us the votes to change our pathetic Immigration Laws! Remember the Midterms!" (Cadelago and Hesson 2018). After Democrats gained control of the House in the midterms, however, Trump quickly dropped all references to the migrant caravan. Instead, he turned his attention to pressuring the outgoing Congress to appropriate funds to construct a wall along the 1,900-mile length of the U.S.–Mexico border, creating a budget impasse that led to a lengthy federal government shutdown.

Preelection Focus on Migrant Caravan

Trump and his advisers devised their strategy aimed at preserving the Republican congressional majority based on polls showing that illegal immigration and border security held strong importance for voters in competitive swing districts. The migrant caravan—which consisted of between 3,500 and 7,000 men, women, and children fleeing poverty and violence in Central America—offered a dramatic visual representation of what Trump called an "assault" or "invasion" of the country's borders by mobs of unscrupulous people hoping to take advantage of lax security and lenient asylum laws. He stoked fears about the caravan in an effort to activate his political base on behalf of Republican candidates. "The vast majority of Americans worry that our border isn't secure, and that criminals, gangs, and drugs are coming into the country across the border," said Republican pollster Chris Wilson, "and the images of this mass of people basically tearing down fences to enter Mexico only reinforce those concerns" (Cadelago and Hesson 2018).

In appearances at campaign rallies for Republican candidates, Trump derided Democrats as weak on immigration and insisted that American voters needed a Republican Congress to protect them from evildoers trying to enter the country. "If Democrats get elected they will do everything in their power to dismantle ICE; they want to turn America into a giant sanctuary city for violent predators and ruthless gang members," he said at a Florida event. "We will keep the criminals, drug dealers, terrorists the hell out of our country" (Fritze and Jackson 2018). Returning to themes from his presidential campaign—in which he described Mexican immigrants as criminals and rapists—Trump characterized the Central American migrants as an imminent threat to national security. "That's an invasion. I don't care what they say. I don't care what the fake media says.

That's an invasion of our country," he declared at a rally in Tennessee. "I am telling the caravans, the criminals, the smugglers, the trespassers marching toward our border, turn back now, because you are not getting in. Turn back" (Scott 2018).

The Department of Homeland Security (DHS) posted a fact sheet online claiming that it had identified more than 270 individuals with known criminal histories "along the caravan route" and asserting that the "flow" of migrants toward the border contained individuals from more than 20 countries. A *Washington Post* fact-checker criticized the post for its vague wording and argued that DHS had extrapolated the figures from historic data about all border crossers (Kessler 2018). In an October 22 tweet, Trump claimed that dangerous "Middle Easterners" and potential terrorists had infiltrated the migrant caravan. "You got some bad people in those groups. You got some tough people in those groups," he declared. "And I'll tell you what—this country doesn't want them. OK? We don't want them" (Haberman and Landler 2018). The following day, however, Trump admitted that he had no evidence to back up his statement. "There's no proof of anything," he said. "But they could very well be" (Gomez 2018). Trump also came under criticism for retweeting a political ad that combined footage of the migrant caravan with shots of an undocumented immigrant who was convicted of murdering two law enforcement officers in California. Critics condemned the ad as misleading and racist.

In addition to ramping up his rhetoric about the migrant caravan, Trump also made it the focus of several policy initiatives in the weeks leading up to the 2018 election. He sent 7,000 U.S. Army and National Guard troops to the southern border, for instance, where they assisted U.S. Customs and Border Protection (CBP) agents in constructing tent cities and erecting barbed-wire fencing. Trump also threatened to cut off $500 million in foreign aid to El Salvador, Guatemala, and Honduras if their governments did not take action to prevent migrant caravans from forming and approaching the United States. Critics pointed out that U.S. aid helped fund many programs to alleviate poverty, crime, corruption, and other problems in the Northern Triangle countries, so withdrawing such assistance would likely worsen conditions and cause more citizens to flee and seek asylum. Trump also threatened to close the U.S.–Mexico border and rescind regional trade agreements if Mexican President Enrique Peña Nieto did not stop the migrant caravan. Although Peña Nieto sent Mexican police to intercept the caravan and offered the migrants incentives to remain in Mexico, most caravan members continued on toward the United States.

Trump's relentless focus on immigration proved effective in inciting nationalist fervor and racial animus among his base. He convinced some Republican voters that the migrant caravan—which remained hundreds of miles south of the U.S.–Mexico border on election day—posed an imminent threat to invade their neighborhoods and disrupt their lives. A 75-year-old woman from Minnesota, for instance, told reporters she worried about migrant gangs taking over her summer lake house. "What's to stop them?" she asked. "We have a lot of people who live on lakes in the summer and winter someplace else. When they come back in the spring, their house would be occupied" (Scott 2018). Trump consistently blamed his political opponents for what he described as an immigration crisis. "The Democrats don't care what their extremist immigration agenda will do to your neighborhoods or your hospitals or your schools," he told supporters at a rally in Houston (Cadelago and Hesson 2018).

Throughout the campaign, Democrats, mainstream media analysts, and immigrant rights advocates accused Trump of propagating exaggerations and falsehoods about the migrant caravan to distract the electorate from valid concerns about his policies and conduct. Critics asserted that the caravan consisted mainly of Central American women and children seeking asylum rather than criminals, gang members, and terrorists. They noted that when a 523-member migrant caravan arrived at the border in April 2018, only 122 members attempted to enter the country illegally, while 401 members presented themselves at ports of entry and requested asylum in accordance with international law. Among the asylum seekers, 93 percent successfully passed an initial interview to determine whether they faced a credible fear of persecution or violence in their home countries. "There is absolutely no reason to further politicize and militarize this humanitarian crisis," said Representative Adam Smith (D-WA) (Gomez 2018).

As evidence that Trump engaged in fearmongering about the migrant caravan for political gain, opponents pointed out that the president suddenly dropped the subject as soon as the election was over. After tweeting about the caravan 34 times—or more than twice per day—during the last two weeks of October, Trump never brought it up after Election Day (Gomez 2018). In fact, the president became angry when CNN White House correspondent Jim Acosta raised the topic in a press conference. When Acosta asked Trump whether he had "demonized immigrants" by characterizing the caravan as an invasion, Trump responded by calling Acosta a "rude, terrible person," falsely accusing him of shoving a White House intern who tried to grab his microphone, and revoking his press pass (Wang and Farhi 2018). "I've never before seen an American president, after going all over the country about this national crisis, then the day after an election shrug," said presidential historian Douglas Brinkley. "It was a dangerous form of xenophobia, aimed solely for electoral purposes, and had nothing to do in the end with real national security" (Haberman and Landler 2018).

The migrant caravan finally reached the U.S.–Mexico border a few weeks after the election. Although thousands of caravan members sought asylum in the United States, the Trump administration refused to allow them to enter the country. Instead, they were forced to stay in overcrowded, makeshift shelters in the Mexican border city of Tijuana while they awaited their asylum interviews—a process that could take weeks or months. On November 25, mounting frustration and desperation led several hundred migrants to stage a protest march and attempt to cross the border to San Diego illegally. CBP officers turned back the migrants by firing tear gas canisters and temporarily closing the busy San Ysidro border crossing. Immigrant rights advocates criticized the CBP response as overly aggressive and violent. "Tear gas across the border against unarmed families is a new low," Senator Brian Schatz (D-HI) posted on Twitter (Averbuch and Malkin 2018). DHS Secretary Kirstjen Nielsen defended the CBP's actions, claiming that the migrants had thrown rocks and projectiles at border agents and had employed women and children as human shields to generate sympathy.

Postelection Focus on Border Wall Funding

Despite Trump's efforts, the results of the 2018 midterms gave the Democratic Party control of the U.S. House of Representatives for the first time since 2010. Democrats picked up 40 seats—far more than the 23 needed for a majority—and won the popular vote by a margin of 8.6 points, which equated to 10 million more votes for House Democrats than House Republicans. Some political analysts described the Democratic gains as a "blue wave," referring to the color typically used to represent the party on electoral maps. The results of several key races suggested that voters had rejected Trump's hardline immigration policies. In the Arizona Senate race, for example, Democratic candidate Krysten Sinema defeated Republican candidate Martha McSally, who had echoed Trump's warnings about the migrant caravan during her campaign.

Facing the prospect of working with a divided Congress for the first time, Trump shifted focus during the lame-duck session toward obtaining funding for his border wall. Although erecting a physical barrier between the United States and Mexico had always formed the cornerstone of Trump's strategy for ending illegal immigration, he made little progress toward that goal during the first two years of his presidency. Following the 2018 midterms, Trump demanded that the outgoing Republican-controlled Congress approve $5.7 billion for the wall as part of the appropriations bill to fund federal government operations for 2019. On December 11, during a contentious, televised Oval Office meeting with Democratic congressional leaders Nancy Pelosi (D-CA) and Chuck Schumer (D-NY), Trump threatened to shut down the federal government if they did not include wall funding in the annual budget. "If we don't get what we want," he warned, "I am proud to shut down the government for border security" (Everett, Ferris, and Oprysko 2018).

When the two sides failed to reach a deal by the December 22 deadline for passing appropriations legislation, federal departments and agencies that provided nonessential services were forced to shut down operations, affecting 800,000 employees as well as millions of Americans who utilized government services. Although Trump attempted to blame Democrats for the government shutdown, a majority of Americans remembered the president's earlier statements and held him responsible. In a CBS News poll, 71 percent of respondents said building a wall on the border was not important enough to justify shutting down the federal government, and 66 percent said Trump should approve budget legislation that did not include wall funding. The poll also showed that Trump's public approval ratings dropped three points from November to reach a new low of 36 percent, while 59 percent of Americans disapproved of the president's job performance (Salvanto et al. 2019).

During the shutdown, Trump and congressional Republicans offered several deals in an effort to secure funding for the border wall. They proposed a temporary extension of the DACA program, for instance, as well as restoration of Temporary Protected Status (TPS) for citizens of certain countries designated as unsafe due to political instability, ethnic strife, armed conflict, or natural disaster. Republican budget proposals also included changes to immigration policy that would make it more difficult for migrant children from Central America to seek asylum, however, by requiring them to apply from their home countries and limiting applications to minors with a "qualified" parent already in the United States. Although Republican leaders presented it as a compromise, Congressional Democrats quickly rejected the deal. "The president's proposal is one-sided, harshly partisan, and was made in bad faith," Schumer stated. "The asylum changes are a poison pill, if there ever was one" (Rose 2019).

The government shutdown remained in place until January 25, when growing public pressure and sagging approval ratings convinced Trump to sign a stopgap bill to reopen the federal government through February 15. Trump also threatened to bypass Congress and obtain funding for the border wall by declaring a national emergency, which he claimed would give him the power to divert money from other sources, such as the military budget and disaster-relief funds. Shortly before the new budget deadline expired, Trump signed an appropriations bill to fund federal government operations through the end of the fiscal year. The legislation only included $1.375 billion to construct new fencing along 55 miles of the U.S.–Mexico border.

At the same time, Trump declared a national emergency in an attempt to gain access to $8 billion for border security. Political opponents vowed to challenge the action in court, accusing the president of manufacturing a crisis in order to subvert Congress's budgetary authority. In a joint statement, Pelosi and Schumer described the national emergency declaration as "a lawless act, a gross abuse of the power of the presidency, and a desperate attempt to distract from the fact that President Trump broke his core promise to have Mexico pay for his wall. . . . This is not an emergency, and the president's fearmongering doesn't make it one" (Pramuk and Wilkie 2019). Even some Republicans expressed concerns about Trump's unilateral action, arguing that it established a dangerous precedent that could allow future Democratic presidents to fund their own policy priorities without congressional approval.

Further Reading

Averbuch, Maya, and Elisabeth Malkin. 2018. "Migrants in Tijuana Run to U.S. Border, but Fall Back in the Face of Tear Gas." *New York Times*, November 25, 2018. https://www.nytimes.com/2018/11/25/world/americas/tijuana -mexico-border.html.

Cadelago, Christopher, and Ted Hesson. 2018. "Why Trump Is Talking Nonstop about the Migrant Caravan." *Politico*, October 23, 2018. https://www .politico.com/story/2018/10/23/trump-caravan-midterm-elections -875888.

Department of Homeland Security. 2018. "Myth vs. Fact: Caravan." DHS.gov, November 1, 2018. https://www.dhs.gov/news/2018/11/01/myth-vs-fact -caravan.

Everett, Burgess, Sarah Ferris, and Caitlin Oprysko. 2018. "Trump Says He's 'Proud' to Shut Down Government during Fight with Pelosi and Schumer." *Politico*, December 11, 2018. https://www.politico.com/story /2018/12/11/trump-border-wall-congress-budget-1055433.

Fritze, John, and David Jackson. 2018. "Donald Trump Hammers on Immigration, Caravan in Final Rallies before Midterm Election." *USA Today*,

November 3, 2018. https://www.usatoday.com/story/news/politics/elections /2018/11/03/midterm-elections-2018-donald-trump-hammers -immigration-message/1881561002/.

Gomez, Alan. 2018. "Tracking Trump's Many Threats, Claims on Immigration, Caravan Ahead of Midterm Elections." *USA Today*, November 1, 2018. https://www.usatoday.com/story/news/politics/elections/2016/2018/11 /01/donald-trump-immigration-migrant-caravan-central-america -asylum-midterm-elections/1846817002/.

Haberman, Maggie, and Mark Landler. 2018. "A Week after the Midterms, Trump Seems to Forget the Caravan." *New York Times*, November 13, 2018. https://www.nytimes.com/2018/11/13/us/politics/trump-caravan -midterms.html.

Kessler, Glenn. 2018. "The Trump Administration's Fuzzy Math about 'Criminals' in the Caravan." *Washington Post*, November 9, 2018. https://www .washingtonpost.com/politics/2018/11/09/trump-administrations-fuzzy -math-criminals-caravan/.

Pramuk, Jacob, and Christina Wilkie. 2019. "Trump Declares National Emergency to Build Border Wall, Setting Up Massive Legal Fight." CNBC, February 15, 2019. https://www.cnbc.com/2019/02/15/trump-national -emergency-declaration-border-wall-spending-bill.html.

Rose, Joel. 2019. "The Border Wall Isn't the Only Reason Democrats Oppose Plan to End the Shutdown." NPR, January 22, 2019. https://www.npr.org /2019/01/22/687516967/the-border-wall-isnt-the-only-reason-democrats -oppose-plan-to-end-the-shutdown.

Salvanto, Anthony, Jennifer De Pinto, Fred Backus, and Kabir Khanna. 2019. "Pelosi Has Edge over Trump on Budget Negotiations, CBS News Poll Shows." CBS News, January 23, 2019. https://www.cbsnews.com/news /pelosi-has-edge-over-trump-on-budget-negotiations-says-cbs-news-poll/.

Scott, Eugene. 2018. "Before the Midterms, Trump Harped on the Migrant Caravan. Since Then, He Hasn't Brought It Up." *Washington Post*, November 8, 2018. https://www.washingtonpost.com/politics/2018/11/08 /before-midterms-trump-harped-migrant-caravan-since-then-he-has -barely-mentioned-it/.

Wang, Amy B., and Paul Farhi. 2018. "White House Suspends Press Pass of CNN's Jim Acosta after His Testy Exchange with Trump." *Washington Post*, November 8, 2018. https://www.washingtonpost.com/politics/2018 /11/08/white-house-suspends-press-pass-cnns-jim-acosta-after-testy -exchange-with-trump/.

The Trump Administration Continues Separating Families (2019)

President Donald Trump's zero tolerance policy, which resulted in the separation of more than 2,000 migrant families crossing the U.S.–Mexico border in the spring of 2018, ended quickly in the face of public outrage, political backlash, and legal repercussions. Trump issued an executive order revoking the controversial policy on June 20, and six days later U.S. district court judge Dana M. Sabraw ordered the government to reunite all the migrant parents and children who had been separated under it. The judge also issued an injunction prohibiting further family separations "unless there is a determination that the parent is unfit or presents a danger to the child" (Jarrett 2018). It soon became clear, however, that U.S. immigration officials continued to separate migrant children from their parents long after Trump promised to shift his administration's focus toward maintaining family unity.

Kevin McAleenan, who became acting secretary of the Department of Homeland Security (DHS) following the resignation of Kirstjen Nielsen, described the ongoing family separations as "extraordinarily rare" and said they only occurred when necessary to protect migrant children's health or safety. He claimed that the process was "carefully governed by policy and by court order" to serve the children's best interests (Sacchetti 2019a). Immigrant rights advocates asserted that family separations occurred much more frequently than immigration officials admitted, however, and often proceeded with questionable justification. They argued that the Trump administration exploited the "child welfare" loophole in Sabraw's ruling to continue its cruel and inhumane treatment of migrant families. "When [family separation] happened under prior administrations there were usually strong indicators of real and legitimate child welfare concerns," said Attorney Lisa Koop of the National Immigrant Justice Center. "What we're seeing right now is of an entirely different character. These are gratuitous separations" (Kriel and Begley 2019).

Separation for Minor Offenses and Health Conditions

As interpreted by court rulings and implemented by previous administrations, the rationale for immigration authorities to remove migrant children from the custody of their parents or guardians involved serious threats to the children's health or safety. If immigration officials suspected that unrelated adults were falsely claiming a family relationship with a child, for instance, they might remove the child to prevent potential trafficking. Border agents might also take children away from parents determined to be unfit to care for them due to charges of domestic violence, sexual abuse, endangerment, or neglect. Immigration authorities occasionally removed children perceived to be at risk from a parent's involvement in criminal activity or gang violence. Finally, border agents sometimes separated migrant children from parents placed in quarantine to prevent the spread of communicable diseases.

Lawyers for the American Civil Liberties Union (ACLU)—whose lawsuit challenging the Trump administration's family separation policies had produced the injunction—claimed that immigration officials removed 911 migrant children from their parents within a year after the practice supposedly ended. Around 20 percent, or 182, of the children affected by the new separations were under age five. According to government records, 74 percent of the separations occurred because the migrant parent allegedly had a criminal record or gang affiliation (Sacchetti 2019a). In some cases, the migrant parents were not informed why they were separated from their children or where their children were taken. Approximately 300 of the 911 children ended up in the care of Catholic Charities' Unaccompanied Refugee Minors Program. As of July 2019, the organization reported that only 3 of those children had been reunited with their parents, while 33 were returned to their home countries and 185 were placed with other relatives or sponsors in the United States (Spagat and Galvan 2019).

After reviewing the case files for the 911 children, the ACLU attorneys found many family separations based on minor offenses, such as traffic tickets, disorderly conduct, property damage, petty theft, or marijuana possession. Some of the files did not provide details about the alleged crimes, while others cited charges that had been resolved years or decades earlier. Some of the information about gang affiliation or criminal activity appeared to come from foreign law enforcement or military records of dubious accuracy. "It is shocking that the Trump administration continues to take babies from their parents," said ACLU attorney Lee Gelernt. "The administration must not be allowed to circumvent the court order over infractions like minor traffic violations" (Spagat and Galvan 2019).

The ACLU filed a complaint asking Sabraw to review the recent family separations and determine whether they fell within the limits established in his earlier ruling. The attorneys noted several specific cases in which U.S. law would prohibit the removal of American children from the custody of their parents based on the same minor offense or unverified accusation. In one case, a border agent separated a one-year-old girl from her father because he allowed her to sleep in a wet diaper. Immigration officials also removed a malnourished two-year-old Guatemalan girl from her father due to "neglect," despite his explanation that they had come to the United States to escape from extreme poverty and food shortages. A father with a disability affecting his speech lost custody of his four-year-old son because he was unable to answer questions from immigration officials.

The ACLU court filing asserted that migrant parents lost custody of their children for past convictions for minor crimes, such as driving with an expired license or destruction of property valued at $5. A woman from El Salvador was separated from her three-year-old son after border agents accused her of gang affiliation. The mother and her child remained apart for three months until her attorney located documents proving that she had been a victim of gang violence rather than a gang member. In some cases, immigration officials justified family separation on the basis of dubious health concerns. One migrant child was shipped to a facility for unaccompanied minor refugees in New York when her mother underwent surgery for a broken leg in California. A Honduran man whose wife died of AIDS lost custody of his three young daughters because he acknowledged being HIV positive. "The government is trying to drive a truck through what was supposed to be a very narrow exception," Gelernt stated. "The government is unilaterally deciding parents are a danger and then separating them . . . without affording any due process to the family" (Kriel and Begley 2019).

In addition, ACLU lawyers noted that the 911 family separations recorded by U.S. immigration officials only covered situations involving parents and children. They contended that the Trump administration routinely separated migrant children from members of their extended families—including grandparents, aunts, uncles, cousins, siblings, and stepparents—without recording these instances as family separations. Only parents and children met the government's definition of legal family units. Children who crossed the border with other relatives—often seeking to reunite with parents already in the United States—were placed in the category of "family relationship in question," separated from their relatives, and treated as unaccompanied minors. The Trump administration maintained that the ACLU lawsuit and court injunction did not apply to extended families, so it did not track those cases as family separations. Anecdotal evidence from organizations that shelter refugee children suggested that hundreds or even thousands of additional migrant children may have been removed from the care of relatives since the official end of the family separation policy, but immigration officials refused to provide exact figures. "They don't want anybody to hold them accountable," said Representative Joaquin Castro (D-TX), chair of the Congressional Hispanic Caucus. "You have an administration determined to get away with what they can and to test the legal limits" (O'Toole 2019).

Fake Families and Fraudulent Asylum Claims

The ongoing separation of families occurred as the Trump administration struggled to deal with a surge of Central American migrants crossing the southern border. In March 2019, for instance, U.S. Customs and Border Patrol (CBP) agents apprehended more than 92,600 people—an increase of 148 percent from a year earlier and the highest monthly total in more than a decade. Families traveling with children accounted for 57 percent of those captured. Administration officials blamed the Flores Settlement Agreement (FSA) and other laws restricting the government's ability to hold minors in immigration detention, claiming that they provided a powerful incentive for migrants to bring children across the border in hopes of being released into the United States to await immigration hearings. "The only way to change the trend is to change the message that if you bring a child, you'll be allowed into our country," said Brian Hastings, head of CBP law enforcement operations (Morrissey 2019).

Most of the migrants arriving from the Northern Triangle countries of Central America requested asylum in the United States. Asylum is a form of protection granted by national governments to refugees who demonstrate a credible fear of persecution, torture, or violence in their home countries. By 2019, 1 out of every 3 people crossing the southern border sought to initiate the asylum process, compared to 1 out of every 100 a decade earlier (Sacchetti 2019b). The increase in asylum claims created huge backlogs in immigration courts as well as severe overcrowding in immigration detention facilities. Trump often expressed frustration with asylum laws, arguing that they encouraged migrants to make fraudulent claims and hampered his ability to secure the border and prevent illegal immigration.

Administration officials asserted that many of the so-called families seeking asylum consisted of unrelated adults who brought children across the border to increase their chances of being allowed to remain in the United States. Trump accused asylum seekers of lying about conditions in their home countries in order to perpetrate a "hoax" or a "big fat con job" on the U.S. immigration system. He also claimed that gang members, criminals, and "rough, tough people" were exploiting children and taking advantage of loopholes in immigration laws (O'Toole 2019). CBP officials reportedly identified more than 3,100 "fraudulent families" attempting to cross the border between April 2018 and March 2019. Trump argued that his family separation policy served as a deterrent to prevent such abuses. "Once you don't have it, that's why you see many more people coming," he said. "They're coming like it's a picnic, because, 'Let's go to Disneyland'" (O'Toole 2019).

Immigrant rights advocates pointed out that the number of "fraudulent families" represented less than 1 percent of the 400,000 families apprehended at the border in the year following Sabraw's ruling. In addition, they asserted that immigration officials often counted children traveling with relatives other than their parents toward these totals (Kriel and Begley 2019). Finally, immigration attorneys found many cases in which migrant children were separated from their parents either by mistake or as a means of pressuring the parents to give up asylum claims and return to their home countries. A Guatemalan farmer named Tomas, for instance, sought asylum with his 14-year-old son after gang members killed several of their relatives. Upon their arrival at the U.S. border, agents accused them of falsifying records and lying about their relationship. "Immigration told me that he wasn't my son," Tomas recalled. "I said, 'He is my son. We can do a blood test. I have his birth certificate.' But they didn't listen to me" (Sacchetti 2019b). Immigration officials detained Tomas in California and sent his son to a shelter for unaccompanied minors in Chicago. After three months apart, they decided to return to Guatemala together rather than live separately in the United States for the duration of their asylum proceedings.

Although child welfare advocates recognized the need to protect migrant children from the risk of trafficking, they insisted that separating children from family members also caused lasting harm. The Young Center for Immigrant Children's Rights represented 120 children affected by the Trump administration's family separation policies and determined the separations to be "contrary to the best interests of the child" in nearly every case. "DHS officials with no child welfare expertise are making split-second decisions, and these decisions have traumatic, lifelong consequences for the children and their families," said Jennifer Nagda, the organization's policy director (Sacchetti 2019a).

Further Reading

Goldberg, Michelle. 2019. "The Terrible Things Trump Is Doing in Our Name." *New York Times*, June 21, 2019. https://www.nytimes.com/2019/06/21/opinion/family-separation-trump-migrants.html.

Jarrett, Laura. 2018. "Federal Judge Orders Reunification of Parents and Children, End to Most Family Separations at Border." CNN, June 27, 2018. https://www.cnn.com/2018/06/26/politics/federal-court-order-family-separations/index.html.

Kriel, Lomi, and Dug Begley. 2019. "Trump Administration Still Separating Hundreds of Migrant Children at the Border through Often Questionable Claims of Danger." *Houston Chronicle*, June 22, 2019. https://www.houston

chronicle.com/news/houston-texas/houston/article/Trump-admin
istration-still-separating-hundreds-of-14029494.php.

Morrissey, Kate. 2019. "Border Apprehensions Reached Decade High in March."
San Diego Union-Tribune, April 9, 2019. https://www.sandiegouniontribune
.com/news/immigration/story/2019-04-09/border-apprehensions
-reached-decade-high-in-march.

O'Toole, Molly. 2019. "Family Separations a Year Later: The Fallout—And the
Separations—Continue." *Los Angeles Times*, April 19, 2019. https://www
.latimes.com/politics/la-na-pol-family-separation-trump-year-later
-20190412-story.html.

Sacchetti, Maria. 2019a. "ACLU: U.S. Has Taken Nearly 1,000 Child Migrants
from Their Parents since Judge Ordered Stop to Border Separations."
Washington Post, July 30, 2019. https://www.washingtonpost.com/immi
gration/aclu-us-has-taken-nearly-1000-child-migrants-from-their-parents
-since-judge-ordered-stop-to-border-separations/2019/07/30/bde452d8
-b2d5-11e9-8949-5f36ff92706e_story.html.

Sacchetti, Maria. 2019b. "U.S. Asylum Process Is at the Center of Trump's Immigration Ire." *Washington Post*, April 9, 2019. https://www.washingtonpost
.com/immigration/us-asylum-process-is-at-the-center-of-trumps
-immigration-ire/2019/04/09/7f8259b8-5aec-11e9-842d-7d3ed7eb3957
_story.html.

Spagat, Elliot, and Astrid Galvan. 2019. "ACLU: 911 Children Split at Border
since 2018 Court Order." *AP News*, July 31, 2019. https://apnews.com/ba
5a05e6a7f14b6b898d75712dee1f6b.

Activists Expose Migrant Child Detention Conditions (2019)

Even after President Donald Trump revoked his controversial family
separation policy, immigration officials continued to detain migrant
children who entered the United States unaccompanied or with adult
relatives other than their parents. Beginning in the spring of 2019, a
series of reports raised concerns about conditions in migrant detention
facilities operated by federal immigration agencies—especially those
that held children. Immigrant rights activists, doctors, progressive lawmakers, journalists, and other observers described traumatized children
crowded into "cages" made of chain-link fencing, sleeping on concrete
floors under thin Mylar blankets, and lacking access to hot meals, basic
hygiene items, medical care, and adult supervision. Immigration attorneys argued that the circumstances and duration of many child detentions violated the Flores Settlement Agreement (FSA), which required
U.S. government agencies to house minors in "safe and sanitary" conditions. Other critics asserted that the government's treatment of migrant

children amounted to intentional cruelty, neglect, and denial of fundamental human rights.

Trump called the reports of deplorable conditions at border detention centers "phony and exaggerated" and insisted that federal immigration agencies were "doing a great job" under difficult circumstances (Jones 2019). Although the president acknowledged that detention facilities were crowded, he blamed Democrats in Congress for refusing to reform outdated immigration laws that he claimed provided incentives for families and unaccompanied minors to cross the border. Trump also demanded that Congress approve humanitarian funding to help immigration agencies deal with unprecedented numbers of migrants in custody. In fiscal year 2019, U.S. border patrol agents apprehended more than 851,500 people attempting to cross the southern border without authorization—more than double the total from a year earlier. Families traveling with children accounted for nearly 56 percent of those apprehended, while unaccompanied minors accounted for 9 percent (U.S. Customs and Border Protection 2019).

Coping with an Influx of Migrant Children

The large numbers of migrants seeking to enter the United States, coupled with the high percentage of children and family units, created significant challenges for federal immigration agencies. U.S. Customs and Border Protection (CBP)—the federal law enforcement agency charged with maintaining border security—detained migrants on a short-term basis in processing centers near the border until they could be returned to their home countries or transferred to the custody of other government agencies. CBP officials noted that these facilities were equipped to hold up to 4,000 people per day. Between May 14 and June 13, 2019, however, U.S. Border Patrol facilities housed an average of 14,000 people per day, including around 2,000 children who either crossed the border unaccompanied or were separated from adult relatives (Lind 2019).

Following apprehension and processing by CBP, adult migrants were typically transferred to the custody of U.S. Immigration and Customs Enforcement (ICE) to await legal proceedings for deportation or asylum. ICE operated immigration detention centers across the country and also contracted to use available space in county jails and privately owned prisons. Although Congress established an average daily limit of 45,000 people in ICE custody for fiscal 2019, the agency set a new record of 52,400 individuals in detention in mid-May 2019. Critics contended that Trump's aggressive enforcement of immigration laws overloaded the system and contributed to the poor treatment of detainees. "This is an avoidable humanitarian crisis manufactured by the Trump administration's harsh policies, which are driven by the president's extreme rhetoric and distorted assessments of the migrant population," said former senior ICE official Kevin Landy (Aleaziz 2019).

Different legal standards applied to the detention of unaccompanied migrant children. Under the terms of the FSA and other federal laws, children apprehended at the border could only be kept in CBP detention for 72 hours before being transferred to one of 170 shelters nationwide run by the Office of Refugee Resettlement (ORR) within the Department of Health and Human Services (HHS) or released to the care of relatives or other sponsors in the community. The Flores agreement also required the government to provide unaccompanied migrant children with safe and sanitary conditions, house them in the least-restrictive setting possible, and make prompt and continuous efforts to reunite them with family members. "That hasn't been happening," according to Dara Lind of Vox. "Attorneys, doctors, and human rights observers have consistently reported that children are being held by Border Patrol for days or longer before being picked up by HHS. And in the meantime, they're being kept in facilities that weren't built to hold even adults for that period of time" (Lind 2019).

Immigration attorneys monitoring the federal government's compliance with the FSA raised some of the first alarms about conditions in CBP detention facilities. Internal inspections within the Department of Homeland Security (DHS), which oversaw both CBP and ICE, also revealed serious issues. In the spring of 2019, the DHS Office of the Inspector General (OIG) released the first in a series of reports expressing concern about severe overcrowding and other problems that posed "an immediate risk to the health and safety" of both detainees and immigration officials at CBP and ICE facilities (Office of the Inspector General 2019). Human rights groups such as the Southern Poverty Law Center conducted their own investigations, while progressive lawmakers, medical practitioners, and journalists also visited detention facilities, interviewed detainees, and publicized their findings.

The reports that emerged painted a deeply disturbing picture of the conditions endured by migrant children in federal custody. Observers found traumatized children dressed in filthy clothing covered with mucus, urine, and feces. Many children reported being denied access to showers and personal hygiene items, such as soap and toothbrushes. "The stench of the children's dirty clothing was so strong it spread to the agents' own clothing—people in town would scrunch their noses when they left work," according to CBP whistleblowers who spoke to the *New York Times* (Editorial Board 2019). In some facilities, investigators saw children as young as ten caring for toddlers without adult assistance. Several facilities experienced outbreaks of lice, scabies, chickenpox, and influenza.

In July 2019, pediatrician Dolly Lucio Sevier examined 38 migrant children being held at a CBP detention center in McAllen, Texas. In a report outlining her findings, she compared the conditions to "torture facilities." Sevier said the young children described "extreme cold temperatures, lights on 24 hours a day, no adequate access to medical care, basic sanitation, water, or adequate food" (ABC News 2019). Some of the children exhibited symptoms of dehydration, malnutrition, sleep deprivation, and psychological trauma. More than two-thirds of those she examined suffered from respiratory illnesses. Sevier attributed their poor health to a lack of basic hygiene in the detention facilities, which she described as "tantamount to intentionally causing the spread of disease" (ABC News 2019).

Immigrant rights advocates claimed that these conditions contributed to the deaths of at least seven children in CBP custody over the course of a year. In comparison, they pointed out that no children had died while in immigration detention in a decade prior to Trump taking office (Acevedo 2019). Administration officials argued that many migrant children endured poverty, malnutrition, and arduous journeys before reaching the U.S. border, which may have contributed to the children's deaths by leaving them vulnerable to communicable diseases or underlying health conditions. CBP officials also asserted that the agency's "short-term holding facilities were not designed to hold vulnerable populations," such as young children, and insisted that agency personnel aimed to "provide the best care possible to those in our custody" (Raff 2019). Trump placed the blame for the deaths of two migrant children, ages seven and eight, on his political opponents. "Any deaths of children or others at the border are strictly the fault of the Democrats and their pathetic immigration policies," he tweeted (Fetters 2019).

Representative Alexandria Ocasio-Cortez (D-NY) toured immigrant detention facilities in Texas with a group of progressive lawmakers in July 2019. Detainees told her they had not been allowed to shower for more than two weeks, had been forced to drink out of toilets, and had been subjected to cruelty and psychological abuse by guards. Ocasio-Cortez claimed that the guards had been openly disrespectful toward her and other members of Congress. Shortly after her visit, investigative journalists revealed the existence of a 9,500-member Facebook group in which CBP employees posted jokes about migrant deaths and vulgar memes about Ocasio-Cortez and other critics. Immigrant rights advocates viewed such posts as evidence of a dysfunctional culture within federal immigration agencies that fostered the inhumane treatment of migrants. "For Mr. Trump, deterrence of illegal immigration has been a guiding principle," stated a *New York Times* editorial, "if not by means of a wall, then by means of cruelty toward migrants, from the squalid conditions in detainee facilities to separating children from their parents" (Editorial Board 2019).

Challenging the Definition of "Safe and Sanitary"

Members of the Trump administration denied that conditions within detention facilities were as terrible as reported and accused political opponents of exaggerating the problem. After touring a border detention center in Texas, for instance, Vice President Mike Pence insisted that "every family that I spoke with told me they were being well cared for" (Sergent et al. 2019). A reporter who accompanied Pence, meanwhile, described a horrendous stench emanating from a room so packed with migrants that they had no space to lie down.

Aaron Hull, U.S. Border Patrol chief for the El Paso Sector, acknowledged that the detention facilities were crowded. "We've been talking about overcrowded conditions for some time. That's no secret," he said. "Everyone from us up through the president has talked about that, that it continues to be a problem" (Jones 2019). Hull denied that migrant children lacked access to soap and toothbrushes, however, and claimed that many detainees did not know how to practice proper hygiene. "We can take them to the shower, and we can put them there, but we can't physically make them shower," he stated. "It's the same thing with brushing their teeth. We encounter children who've never brushed their teeth" (Jones 2019).

Trump blamed Democrats in Congress for not approving humanitarian funding to help CBP and other immigration agencies deal with the influx of families and unaccompanied minors crossing the border. Some lawmakers supported bills that earmarked funding to improve detention conditions and speed up processing of asylum applications. Progressive Democrats, including Ocasio-Cortez, opposed any additional funding for border security, arguing that the Trump administration could resolve the crisis by eliminating its harsh immigration policies. "Even an administration acting with the best interests of children in mind at every turn would be scrambling right now," Lind explained. "But policymakers are split on how much of the current crisis is simply a resource problem—one Congress could help by sending more resources—and how much is deliberate mistreatment or neglect from an administration that doesn't deserve any more money or trust" (Lind 2019). Congress eventually passed a spending bill that authorized $4.6 billion to improve conditions at border detention facilities, although progressive Democrats argued that it did not do enough to protect unaccompanied minors.

While Trump asked Congress for money to improve border detention conditions, he also directed the Department of Justice (DOJ) to mount a legal challenge to the FSA, which established the standards for U.S. government treatment of unaccompanied migrant children in custody. Trump administration officials viewed Flores as an outdated measure that fueled the humanitarian crisis by providing incentives for migrants to bring children across the border. In an effort to dismantle the two-decade-old settlement and eliminate the so-called catch-and-release loophole it created in U.S. immigration law, DOJ lawyers appealed a 2017 court ruling that interpreted the meaning of the "safe and sanitary" provision in Flores. They based the appeal on the premise that the judge had "substantially altered the legal relations of the parties" by outlining specific requirements—including access to toiletries and beds—for detention conditions to be considered "safe and sanitary" (White 2019).

Sarah Fabian, an attorney in the DOJ's Office of Immigration Litigation, presented the Trump administration's argument before the U.S. Court of Appeals for the Ninth Circuit in San Francisco. She attempted to defend conditions in CBP detention facilities by claiming that the original FSA did not explicitly define "safe and sanitary." The three-judge panel responded to Fabian's argument with open contempt. "Granted that the decree doesn't have a list of items that has to be supplied in order to be 'sanitary,'" said Judge A. Wallace Tashima, a Japanese American who was confined to a federal internment camp as a child during World War II. "It's within everybody's common understanding that if you don't have a toothbrush, if you don't have soap, if you don't have a blanket, it's not 'safe and sanitary.' Wouldn't everybody agree to that? Do you agree to that?" (Dickinson 2019).

Although Fabian never denied the necessity of those items, she continued to hedge about whether the FSA obligated the government to supply them to migrant children in detention facilities. "Well, I think it's—I think those are—there's fair reason to find that those things may be part of 'safe and sanitary,'" she replied. Tashima rejected her reasoning. "Not 'may be.' *Are* a part," the judge declared. "Why do you say 'may be'? You mean there are circumstances where a person doesn't need to have a toothbrush, toothpaste, and soap? For days?" (Dickinson 2019). NowThis News posted an edited, four-minute clip of Fabian's court appearance on Twitter. The video went viral, receiving more than 20 million views, and generated widespread public outrage. *Atlantic* contributor Ken White described the DOJ's position as "loathsome" and "morally indefensible" and asserted that the Trump administration "should have expected exactly the reception that it got" in court (White 2019).

To many people who saw the clip of her court appearance, Fabian appeared to be a vocal defender of the Trump administration's treatment of migrant children. She received intense criticism in the media and online and became the target of death threats. In her defense, Fabian pointed out that she had joined the DOJ during the Obama administration and had argued the federal government's case on a wide variety of immigration issues over the years. She claimed that viewers of the viral video mistook her professional argument on a technical point of law for personal opposition to providing basic hygiene items to migrant children. "Whether that's because people saw only certain clips of the argument, or because the nature of oral argument is that sometimes your positions don't come out in full, or because I never articulated some pieces of my argument well enough to make my position clear, I can't say," she wrote. "Probably all of those. I do not believe that's the position I was representing" (Fernandez 2019).

To opponents of Trump's immigration policies, however, Fabian's argument provided yet another example of the administration's disregard for the basic humanity and human rights of migrant children. "We are housing thousands of young people—who have committed no crime except traveling with their parents—in unconscionable conditions. . . . If any parent treated their child the way these children are being treated under the guise of 'protection,' they would likely have their child removed from them and face serious jail time," correspondents Nila Bala and Arthur Rizer wrote in an opinion piece for NBC News. "As a nation, we have long held that children deserve to be protected. In fact, our entire legal system recognizes this moral truth: We ensure that children are not exploited in the workforce through child labor laws; we protect children from predators with a network of sex crime legislation; and we have set different levels of criminal culpability for children based on their youth. Yet when it comes to immigration, these considerations fall apart" (Bala and Rizer 2019).

Further Reading

ABC News. 2019. "Doctor Compares Conditions for Children at Immigrant Holding Centers to 'Torture Facilities.'" *ABC Action News*, June 24, 2019. https://www.abcactionnews.com/news/national/doctor-compares-conditions-for-children-at-immigrant-holding-centers-to-torture-facilities.

Acevedo, Nicole. 2019. "Why Are Migrant Children Dying in U.S. Custody?" NBC News, May 29, 2019. https://www.nbcnews.com/news/latino/why -are-migrant-children-dying-u-s-custody-n1010316.

Aleaziz, Hamed. 2019. "More Than 52,000 People Are Now Being Detained by ICE, an Apparent All-Time High." BuzzFeed News, May 20, 2019. https:// www.buzzfeednews.com/article/hamedaleaziz/ice-detention-record -immigrants-border.

Bala, Nila, and Arthur Rizer. 2019. "Trump's Family Separation Policy Never Really Ended. This Is Why." NBC News, July 1, 2019. https://www .nbcnews.com/think/opinion/trump-s-family-separation-policy-never -really-ended-why-ncna1025376.

Dickinson, Tim. 2019. "Trump Administration Argues Migrant Children Don't Need Soap." *Rolling Stone*, June 20, 2019. https://www.rollingstone.com /politics/politics-news/safe-sanitary-no-soap-beds-court-migrants -trump-850744/.

Editorial Board. 2019. "All Presidents Are Deporters in Chief." *New York Times*, July 13, 2019. https://www.nytimes.com/2019/07/13/opinion/sunday /trump-deportations-immigration.html.

Fernandez, Manny. 2019. "Lawyer Draws Outrage for Defending Lack of Tooth- brushes in Border Detention." *New York Times*, June 25, 2019. https:// www.nytimes.com/2019/06/25/us/sarah-fabian-migrant-lawyer -doj.html.

Fetters, Ashley. 2019. "The Moral Failure of Family Separation." *Atlantic*, January 13, 2019. https://www.theatlantic.com/politics/archive/2019/01/trumps -family-separation-policy-causes-national-outrage/579676/.

Jones, Aria. 2019. "Donald Trump: *New York Times, El Paso Times* Article on Clint Facility 'Big Media Con Job.'" *El Paso Times*, July 8, 2019. https://www .elpasotimes.com/story/news/2019/07/08/clint-border-facility-story -blasted-president-donald-trump-twitter/1673309001/.

Lind, Dara. 2019. "The Horrifying Conditions Facing Kids in Border Detention, Explained." Vox, June 25, 2019. https://www.vox.com/policy-and-politics /2019/6/25/18715725/children-border-detention-kids-cages-immigration.

Office of the Inspector General. 2019. "Management Alert: DHS Needs to Address Dangerous Overcrowding and Prolonged Detention of Children and Adults in the Rio Grande Valley." Department of Homeland Security, July 2, 2019. https://www.oig.dhs.gov/sites/default/files/assets/2019-07 /OIG-19-51-Jul19_.pdf.

Raff, Jeremy. 2019. "What a Pediatrician Saw Inside a Border Patrol Warehouse." *Atlantic*, July 3, 2019. https://www.theatlantic.com/politics/archive/2019 /07/border-patrols-oversight-sick-migrant-children/593224/.

Sergent, Jim, Elinor Aspegren, Elizabeth Lawrence, and Olivia Sanchez. 2019. "Chilling First-Hand Reports of Migrant Detention Centers Highlight Smell of 'Urine, Feces,' Overcrowded Conditions." *USA Today*, July 17, 2019. https://www.usatoday.com/in-depth/news/politics/elections/2019

/07/16/migrant-detention-centers-described-2019-us-government
-accounts/1694638001/.

U.S. Customs and Border Protection. 2019. "Southwest Border Migration FY
2019." Department of Homeland Security, October 29, 2019. https://www
.cbp.gov/newsroom/stats/sw-border-migration/fy-2019.

White, Ken. 2019. "Why a Government Lawyer Argued against Giving Immigrant Kids Toothbrushes." *Atlantic*, June 23, 2019. https://www.theatlantic
.com/ideas/archive/2019/06/why-sarah-fabian-argued-against-giving
-kids-toothbrushes/592366/.

White House. 2019. "President Donald J. Trump Is Taking Action to Close
the Loopholes That Fuel the Humanitarian Crisis on Our Border." Fact
Sheet, August 21, 2019. https://www.whitehouse.gov/briefings-statements
/president-donald-j-trump-taking-action-close-loopholes-fuel-human
itarian-crisis-border/.

CHAPTER THREE

Impacts of Family Separation and the U.S.–Mexico Border Crisis

This chapter examines the impact of the Trump administration's immigration policies on the people affected by them and on American society. It reviews medical evidence showing that migrant children subjected to family separation and detention experience severe and lasting psychological trauma. It also explores how anti-immigrant rhetoric contributes to hostility toward Latinos in the United States, both documented and undocumented. Finally, it analyzes the international response to Trump's immigration policies in the context of a global refugee crisis and presents alternative proposals for immigration reform advanced by 2020 Democratic presidential candidates.

Lasting Trauma for Migrant Children and Families

Some of the most vocal criticism of President Donald Trump's immigration policies came from medical professionals who warned that separating migrant families and detaining migrant children had the potential to cause severe and lasting psychological harm. "The administration's policy of separating children from their families as they attempt to cross into the United States without documentation is not only needless and cruel, it threatens the mental and physical health of both the children and their caregivers," said Jessica Henderson Daniel, president of the American Psychological Association (Stringer 2018). Dozens of organizations representing more than 250,000 doctors—including the American Academy of Pediatrics, the American College of Physicians, and the American Medical Association—issued statements and delivered petitions condemning the administration's treatment of migrant children and families (Wan 2018). "Family unity is recognized as a civil right under the U.S. constitution and under international law," said Kathryn Hampton of Physicians for Human Rights. "Under no circumstances should it be U.S. policy to traumatize children and their families" (Short 2019b).

Mental health experts pointed out that most of the Central American migrants entering the United States sought asylum from violence and persecution in their home countries. They endured a treacherous journey through Mexico in search of protection and safety, only to be subjected to the additional trauma of family separation under the administration's zero tolerance policy. Doctors who examined migrant children separated from their parents at the border identified many immediate signs of psychological harm, including posttraumatic stress, separation anxiety, behavioral regression, and depression. Some experts predicted that the children would continue to experience long-term health effects, leading to what child psychiatrist Gilbert Kliman described as "an epidemic of physical, psychosomatic health problems that are costly to society as well as to the individual child grown up. I call it a vast, cruel experiment on the backs of children" (Long, Mendoza, and Burke 2019).

Even after the Trump administration stopped separating migrant families as a matter of policy, thousands of migrant children—whether unaccompanied or as part of family units—endured prolonged periods of immigration detention after reaching the United States. Nearly 70,000 migrant children spent time in U.S. government custody during fiscal year 2019, a 42 percent increase from the previous year, and they tended to be held for an average of two months, as opposed to one month in 2018 (Sherman, Mendoza, and Burke 2019). Reports from doctors who visited border detention facilities raised serious concerns about overcrowded and unsanitary conditions, noting hundreds of children confined in chain-link "cages," sleeping on concrete floors, and lacking access to clean clothing, soap, toothbrushes, and medical care. Mental health experts argued that even brief exposure to such conditions could create toxic stress in children, which was associated with significant physical and psychological health risks later in life. "There's no amount of time that it's safe for children to be detained," said immigration attorney Neha Desai. "We know definitively that detention harms children; that every single day they're there, those impacts compound" (Taddonio 2019). Despite such risks of lasting harm, however, the Trump administration challenged laws limiting the duration of child detention and proposed new rules allowing for the indefinite detention of migrant families with children.

Family Separation Compounds Trauma

Many analysts attributed the increase in migrant families and unaccompanied minors attempting to cross the U.S.–Mexico border to dangerous conditions in El Salvador, Guatemala, and Honduras—the Northern Triangle countries of Central America. In addition to experiencing widespread poverty, countries in this region struggled to curb the influence of criminal gangs that used intimidation and violence to recruit, exploit, and control children. Corruption in law enforcement and instability in government left citizens without protection from gang violence. Fearing for their lives, many people decided to migrate northward and seek asylum in the United States. "They have come from a place where they have been exposed to incredible turmoil and sometimes very severe trauma—whether the killing of one parent or family member, domestic violence, plus abject poverty," pediatrician Alan Shapiro said of the migrant children he examined. "There is a lack of food, poor living conditions, dangerous neighborhoods—all of that is the baseline of the children we are seeing. It's critical to understand that these are not people looking for a better life, they are looking to flee dangerous environments with no protection" (Wagner 2018).

Many Central American children and families faced additional trauma during the grueling journey through Mexico, from uncertainty about sources of food and shelter to vulnerability to physical assault, sexual abuse, kidnapping, trafficking, or extortion. Child development experts stressed the importance of environmental stability for children, noting that such exposure to constant change and adverse experiences can be profoundly disruptive. "They ride on the top of trains, in the back of trucks, they are exposed to extremes in weather and temperature, there is a lack of food," Shapiro noted. "[This is] ongoing trauma—so in a child already sensitized, it's ratcheting up the level of stress" (Wagner 2018). By the time migrant children arrived at the U.S. border, many already showed signs of weakened physical and emotional states. Instead of finding safety, stability, and protection, however, they became subject to punitive detention policies intended to deter asylum seekers. "If violence is a major factor driving children to seek refuge in the United States," Hampton explained, "harsh border enforcement will not serve as an effective deterrent and will only cause more harm to an already traumatized population" (Short 2019a).

Some researchers argued that the Trump administration's family separation policy compounded the trauma experienced by migrant children by removing them from their sole source of stability and support. They pointed to studies showing that separating children from parents harms the attachment bond, which forms in infancy and provides children with the basic sense of security they need to develop properly. "The special bond between parent and child is imperative to healthy cognitive and mental development," Hampton stated. "Parents help buffer children from extremely stressful and dangerous situations. Without this vital resource, children are at risk of devastating short- and long-term mental and physical harm" (Short 2019b). Researchers found that children tended to respond to sudden separation from a primary caregiver in distinct phases—including protest, despair, and detachment—which affected their ability to reconnect. "Children reunited while they are in the early separation protest phase usually fare well," said researcher Laura Wood. "Children in despair may respond to the reappearance of their parent with hostility or ambivalence, taking many weeks to rebuild their bond. Children who have detached from their parents may reject their approaches or treat them as strangers" (Wood 2018).

Doctors who examined migrant children found that family separation at the border caused as much psychological distress as the persecution and violence that drove asylum seekers from their home countries. "Family separation was on par with beating and torture in terms of its relationship to mental health," noted researcher Jessica Goodkind (Stringer 2018). According to mental health experts, constant exposure to stress hormones can kill neurons in the developing brains of children, causing irreversible changes in brain structure and function. "It affects regions of the brain and functions that have to do with cognition, intellectual process, with judgment, self-regulation, social skills," said psychiatry professor Luis H. Zayas (Chatterjee 2019). Some of the symptoms exhibited by migrant children included changes in eating and sleeping patterns, loss of bowel or bladder control, self-injury behavior, aggression, and detachment. "Some of the kids are resilient, but many of them suffer from complex trauma, attachment problems, depression, generalized anxiety, and social anxiety," said clinical psychologist Suzana Adams. "I see adolescents who still urinate in bed and kids who exhibit self-harming behaviors, like cutting" (Stringer 2018).

Doctors have found that prolonged exposure to extreme stress can also have toxic physical effects on children, causing inflammatory responses, immune system changes, and organ damage. Excessive or chronic stress during childhood has been linked to an increased risk of developing a range of serious health problems later in life, including heart disease, cancer, diabetes, migraines, and autoimmune disorders (Wood 2018). "Physiologically, we are damaging the immune, nervous, and endocrine systems," Shapiro explained. "All these things with prolonged stress without a buffer lead to long-term chronic diseases" (Wagner 2018).

Pediatricians have noted that very young children are most susceptible to the damaging effects of toxic stress because rapid growth and development occurs during infancy and early childhood. Under the Trump administration's family separation policy, the average age of migrant children held in detention without their parents dropped dramatically. Before it took effect, most minors in government custody were teenagers who crossed the border unaccompanied. Afterward, hundreds of small children were placed in detention after being removed from their parents. Most facilities were poorly equipped to handle the increased care needs of tender-age children. For instance, immigration agencies operated under a policy that prohibited adult staff members from holding or touching underage detainees in shelters. Although these policies aimed to protect vulnerable teenagers from inappropriate physical contact, they also prevented staff members from rocking infants or comforting toddlers. "Depriving very young children of physical comfort serves to significantly heighten distress," Wood wrote, adding that "such circumstances clearly increase the risk of undetected, undertreated, exacerbated, and new-onset health conditions" (Wood 2018). Child psychologists also noted that most detention facilities lacked toys, books, and play areas.

In the absence of adult caregivers, observers often saw older migrant children performing parental duties for younger children in detention facilities, including comforting, feeding, bathing, and changing diapers. Psychologists described this process as "parentification" and asserted that the added responsibility of caring for a younger child compounded the trauma and stress endured by migrant children. Clinical psychologist Louise Earley argued that detained migrant children "are not developmentally equipped to deal with the immense task of caring for an infant in any circumstance, least of all these," and "with no effective support, the prospect that they will inflict unintentional harm or actual harm as a result of their frustrations is likely" (Fetters 2019). Research into parentification suggests children forced to care for others experience psychological and emotional harm that persists into adulthood, resulting in an increased risk of such mental health issues as anxiety, depression, eating disorders, and substance abuse.

The body of research on the long-term health impacts of family separation is limited because scientists have long considered it out of bounds as an area of academic study. "Researchers are not allowed to do to children what was being done to children at the border," said child development expert Megan Gunnar. "For the most part, we are not even conducting experiments that force mother-infant separation on nonhuman primates anymore" (Stringer 2018). Prior to the enactment of the Trump administration's policy, most information on the long-term effects of family separation came from historical episodes now considered reprehensible, such as the enslavement of African Americans, the internment of Japanese Americans, and the removal of Native American children to white boarding schools. An Australian study of Aboriginal children separated from their families, for instance, found that they were twice as likely to be arrested as adults than people raised within families (Wan 2018). "If you take the moral, spiritual, even political aspect out of it, from a strictly medical and scientific point of view, what we as a country are doing to these children at the border is unconscionable," said Zayas. "The harm our government is now causing will take a lifetime to undo" (Wan 2018).

Detention Causes Harm to Children

In addition to the children impacted by the family separation policy, thousands more migrant children faced detention at the U.S. border with their parents while awaiting decisions on deportation or asylum. Although some opponents of family separation portrayed family detention as a more humane alternative, mental health experts asserted that any detention had the potential to cause severe and lasting psychological harm to children. Medical student Sarah MacLean conducted an analysis of questionnaires completed by 425 migrant mothers being detained with their children and found that 32 percent of the children exhibited symptoms of emotional distress, including "wanting to cry all the time, wanting to be with [their] mom, conduct problems, such as fighting with other kids, or having temper tantrums, peer problems, so not having a lot of friends, or only wanting to interact with adults." Also, in interviews with 150 child migrant detainees between ages 9 and 17, MacLean found that 17 percent of the children experienced significant symptoms of posttraumatic stress disorder, such as flashbacks, nightmares, anxiety, and hypervigilance (Chatterjee 2019).

Under normal circumstances, parents' stability, support, and protection provide a buffer to shield children from trauma and its harmful psychological effects. Detention produces stress reactions in migrant parents, however, which erodes their mental health and undermines their parenting capacity. Studies have found that mothers in family detention facilities experience levels of fear and hopelessness that make it difficult to comfort their children and maintain a healthy parental relationship. "Parents who are under the stress of detention not only transmit that stress, anxiety, and depression to their children, but their roles as parents are upended," Zayas explained (Chatterjee 2019). Unfamiliar and uncomfortable conditions, unresponsive or uncaring staff, and uncertainty surrounding deportation combine to create a stressful environment for both parents and children. "It's not the normal experience of children to be living behind walls with barbed wires on them," Zayas stated. "There are prison guards who loom large, who are often gruff and not sensitive, because they are prison guards. They're not guardians" (Chatterjee 2019). The detention environment also reduces the authority and control usually vested in parents, further weakening their attachment bond with traumatized children.

U.S. government investigators acknowledged the negative impacts of detention on migrant children, whether they crossed the border unaccompanied, were separated from their parents, or were detained together with family members. The Office of the Inspector General (OIG) within the Department of Health and Human Services conducted interviews with more than 100 mental health clinicians who worked with migrant children detained in 45 shelters operated by the Office of Refugee Resettlement (ORR). In a report issued in September 2019, OIG inspectors described clinical staff members who felt overwhelmed by the large numbers, young ages, and severity of traumatic experiences among the migrant children they treated. "Facilities reported that addressing the needs of separated children was particularly challenging because these children exhibited more fear, feelings of abandonment, and post-traumatic stress than did children who were not separated," said inspector Ann Maxwell (Hasan 2019). Although ORR guidelines recommended a ratio of 1 clinician to 12 migrant children, most staff members reported treating twice that many young patients at a time, which made it difficult to establish trust and provide individualized attention.

The OIG report recommended minimizing the time migrant children spent in detention facilities in order to limit the psychological harm inflicted upon them. "The longer a child stays in some kind of custody, the greater the damage that can be done," Zayas explained, "so the idea is to get them in, screen them, examine them, treat them—do what you can, but get them someplace where they can have a home-like environment, even if it's just a small group home where they can live with other children, but to really stabilize their lives" (Hasan 2019). Mental health experts rejected the idea that detaining migrant children together with their parents or other family members offered a solution to the problem. "Family detention is not a 'kinder' alternative," Wood declared, "and the 'othering' of immigrants and normalization of suffering should never be tolerated. All forms of immigration detention are highly detrimental to children and adults and the many effective alternatives must be considered" (Wood 2018).

Immigrant rights advocates sought to hold the Trump administration legally responsible for causing psychological harm to migrant children through its family separation and child detention policies. In November 2019, U.S. district court judge John A. Kronstadt ruled that administration officials were "aware of the risks associated with family separation" when they implemented the policy, meaning that they knowingly "caused severe mental trauma to parents and their children" (Sherman, Mendoza, and Burke 2019). Kronstadt ordered the government to provide mental health screenings, counseling services, and long-term psychiatric treatment to the migrant families affected by the policy. "You cannot have a policy of deliberately trying to injure a family bond," said Mark Rosenbaum, an attorney who represented migrant families in the case. "Cruelty cannot be part of an enforcement policy, and here it was the cornerstone of the policy" (Jordan 2019).

Trump administration officials argued that family separation occurred as an unfortunate consequence of their decision to enforce U.S. immigration laws by criminally prosecuting anyone caught crossing the border illegally, including parents with children. They claimed that outdated measures such as the Flores Settlement Agreement, which strictly limited the amount of time migrant children could be detained, forced them to separate families. While previous administrations had released both parents and children pending resolution of their immigration hearings, the Trump administration blamed this lenient "catch-and-release" policy for the influx of families and unaccompanied minors attempting to enter the United States. Administration officials claimed that family separation and child detention served as an effective deterrent to these groups. They noted that migrant parents could avoid prosecution and protect their children from harm by remaining in their home countries or seeking asylum in Mexico.

In August 2019, the Trump administration announced a new policy that would replace the Flores agreement and allow for indefinite detention of migrant families. Trump claimed that the policy was intended to protect children from trauma by convincing migrant families not to attempt the difficult journey to the U.S. border. "Very much I have the children on my mind," the president stated. "It bothers me very greatly" (Naylor 2019).

Acting Department of Homeland Security (DHS) secretary Kevin McAleenan asserted that migrant children and families in indefinite detention "will be universally treated with dignity, respect, and special concern in concert with American values," with such amenities as three hot meals per day and access to recreational facilities (Naylor 2019). The medical establishment objected to the new policy, arguing that any detention of children had the potential to inflict lasting psychological harm. "No child belongs in immigration detention, even if they are detained alongside their parents," Hampton wrote on behalf of Physicians for Human Rights. "This administration should immediately adopt community-based alternatives to detention, which are humane and effective, and which lessen trauma experienced by children and families" (Short 2019b). In September 2019, a federal judge issued an order temporarily blocking the policy from taking effect.

Further Reading

Chatterjee, Rhitu. 2019. "Lengthy Detention of Migrant Children May Create Lasting Trauma, Say Researchers." NPR, August 23, 2019. https://www.npr.org/sections/health-shots/2019/08/23/753757475/lengthy-detention-of-migrant-children-may-create-lasting-trauma-say-researchers.

Fetters, Ashley. 2019. "Children Cannot Parent Other Children." *Atlantic*, June 24, 2019. https://www.theatlantic.com/family/archive/2019/06/immigrant-children-border-parentification/592393/.

Hasan, Syeda. 2019. "Report: Migrant Children Coming to the U.S. Were Traumatized after Family Separation." KERA News, September 12, 2019. https://www.keranews.org/post/report-migrant-children-coming-us-were-traumatized-after-family-separation.

Jordan, Miriam. 2019. "U.S. Must Provide Mental Health Services to Families Separated at Border." *New York Times*, November 6, 2019. https://www.nytimes.com/2019/11/06/us/migrants-mental-health-court.html.

Long, Colleen, Martha Mendoza, and Garance Burke. 2019. "'I Can't Feel My Heart': Children Separated from Their Parents at the U.S.-Mexico Border Showed Increased Signs of Post-Traumatic Stress." PBS *Frontline*, September 4, 2019. https://www.pbs.org/wgbh/frontline/article/children-separated-from-their-parents-at-us-mexico-border-showed-increased-signs-of-post-traumatic-stress-us-report-says/.

Naylor, Brian. 2019. "New Trump Policy Would Permit Indefinite Detention of Migrant Families, Children." NPR, August 21, 2019. https://www.npr.org/2019/08/21/753062975/new-trump-policy-would-permit-indefinite-detention-of-migrant-families-children.

Sherman, Christopher, Martha Mendoza, and Garance Burke. 2019. "U.S. Held a Record Number of Migrant Kids in Custody This Year." PBS, November 12,

2019. https://www.pbs.org/wgbh/frontline/article/u-s-held-record-69
-thousand-migrant-children-in-custody-in-2019/.

Short, Kevin. 2019a. "Asylum-Seeking Children from Northern Triangle Suffer Multi-Dimensional, Recurrent, Sustained Trauma." Physicians for Human Rights, June 10, 2019. https://phr.org/news/asylum-seeking -children-from-northern-triangle-suffer-multi-dimensional-recurrent -sustained-trauma/.

Short, Kevin. 2019b. "U.S. Government Confirms Migrant Children Experience Severe Mental Health Issues Following 'Family Separation.'" Physicians for Human Rights, September 4, 2019. https://phr.org/news/u-s-gover nment-confirms-migrant-children-experienced-severe-mental-health -issues-following-family-separation/.

Stringer, Heather. 2018. "Psychologists Respond to a Mental Health Crisis at the Border." American Psychological Association, September 2018. https:// www.apa.org/news/apa/2018/border-family-separation.

Taddonio, Patrice. 2019. "Inside a Shelter Holding Detained Migrant Kids." PBS, November 12, 2019. https://www.pbs.org/wgbh/frontline/article/inside -a-shelter-holding-detained-migrant-kids/.

Wagner, Alex. 2018. "Extinguishing the Beacon of America." *Atlantic*, June 15, 2018. https://www.theatlantic.com/ideas/archive/2018/06/extinguishing -the-beacon-of-america/562880/.

Wan, William. 2018. "What Separation from Parents Does to Children: 'The Effect Is Catastrophic.'" *Washington Post,* June 18, 2018. https://www .washingtonpost.com/national/health-science/what-separation-from -parents-does-to-children-the-effect-is-catastrophic/2018/06/18/.

Wood, Laura. 2018. "Impact of Punitive Immigration Policies, Parent-Child Separation, and Child Detention on the Mental Health and Development of Children." *BMJ Paediatrics* 2 (1): e000338, September 26, 2018. doi:10.1136/bmjpo-2018-000338.

A Hostile Atmosphere for Immigrants

Critics of President Donald Trump's stance on immigration asserted that his rhetoric and policies fed nativist sentiments and created a hostile, anti-immigrant atmosphere in the United States. They claimed that Trump vilified and dehumanized foreign-born people and their descendants by, for example, referring to Mexican border crossers as "animals" and "rapists," characterizing Central American asylum seekers as "an invasion of our country," telling four U.S. congresswomen of color to "go back" to where they came from, banning travel to the United States by citizens of several predominantly Muslim nations, and defending policies that involved separating migrant children from their parents and denying them access to basic hygiene items. Opponents argued that Trump's words and actions stoked fear and bigotry among his followers, shifted the boundaries of acceptable public discourse, and elevated anti-immigrant views into the mainstream. "The words of a president matter," said former vice president and Democratic presidential candidate Joseph Biden. "They can unleash the deepest, darkest forces in this nation. That is what Donald Trump has chosen to do" (Fritze 2019).

Critics charged that Trump's immigration policies and rhetoric seemed designed to fuel racial and ethnic tensions in the United States. "The president is looking to divide Americans along color lines," proclaimed a *New York Times* editorial, "to conjure a zero-sum vision of America in which whites must contend against nonwhites for jobs, wealth, safety, and citizenship" (Editorial Board 2019). Opponents claimed that by nurturing an us-versus-them mentality in his support base, Trump generated racist anger and resentment and encouraged people to express or act upon those feelings. As evidence, they pointed to incidents in which Latinos were accosted for speaking Spanish in public, subjected to racial profiling by immigration enforcement, or targeted for ethnic violence and hate crimes.

Such incidents contributed to perceptions of a hostile atmosphere that made many Latinos feel unsafe living in the United States. One survey of Latino patients in California emergency rooms found that 75 percent of undocumented immigrants and 51 percent of U.S. citizens and legal residents delayed seeking medical treatment due to such concerns. "Statements coming from the administration and the president really do have significant effects on Latino populations," said Robert Rodriguez, an emergency medicine physician and the study's lead author. "Not only have they induced fear in undocumented immigrants, but they have also caused a substantial proportion of Latino citizens to have concerns about their safety" (Reuters 2019). Other studies found that fear of discrimination or deportation made people in Latino communities reluctant to report crimes and utilize public services. Some prominent Latinos vowed to oppose Trump's immigration policies, dispel misinformation and stereotypes, and establish a welcoming atmosphere for racial and ethnic diversity in the United States.

Criticism of Trump's Anti-immigrant Message

Trump placed a strong emphasis on immigration issues from the beginning of his 2016 presidential campaign. In speeches and social media posts, Trump consistently framed both legal and illegal immigration as threats to national security, public safety, and the U.S. economy.

He also asserted that decades of uncontrolled immigration had negatively impacted the nation's demographic makeup and cultural unity. Echoing anti-immigrant crusades of the past, Trump portrayed some immigrants—particularly Latino immigrants from Mexico and Central America and Muslim immigrants from the Middle East—as undesirable or even dangerous. He proposed policies intended to restrict entry by these groups, such as building a wall along the Mexican border and enacting a travel ban targeting Muslim-majority countries. According to the liberal Center for American Progress, "The Trump administration's policy agenda amounts to a rejection of a fundamental American ideal—welcoming immigrants and valuing diversity—in favor of policies that generate fear and xenophobia and call to mind some of the most shameful episodes in the nation's history" (Partelow and Wolgin 2018).

Both during his campaign and after he took office, Trump surrounded himself with advisers known for their hardline positions on immigration issues, including Jeff Sessions (who served as attorney general from February 2017 to November 2018) and senior policy adviser Stephen Miller. The Trump White House also employed individuals associated with such anti-immigrant organizations as the Center for Immigration Studies (CIS) and the Federation for Immigration Reform (FAIR). Trump frequently used inflammatory rhetoric to describe immigrants as gang members, drug dealers, violent criminals, and terrorists. He also portrayed immigrants as stealing jobs from American workers, draining public welfare resources, and conspiring to take over the country. Many critics viewed Trump's immigration positions and policies as racist. In a January 2018 Oval Office meeting, for instance, he expressed a clear preference for admitting white people from Norway over nonwhite people from what he termed "s***hole countries," including El Salvador, Haiti, and Nigeria. "The president," David A. Graham wrote in the *Atlantic*, "cannot seem to see any way that black and brown people from impoverished, disaster-stricken, or violence-torn countries fit into his zero-sum scheme or his overwhelmingly white vision of what America should look like" (Graham 2018).

Critics also accused Trump of racism in July 2019 following a series of social media attacks on four progressive congresswomen of color. Alexandria Ocasio-Cortez (D-NY), Ilhan Omar (D-MN), Ayanna Pressley (D-MA), and Rashida Tlaib (D-MI) joined a group of fellow lawmakers on a tour of immigration detention facilities near the southern border in Texas. Afterward, they held a press conference to publicize the conditions in which migrant families were being held. Ocasio-Cortez said detainees told her they had not been allowed to shower for more than two weeks, had been forced to drink out of toilets, and had been subjected to psychological abuse by guards. Trump responded by saying that his critics should "go back" to "the totally broken and crime infested places from which they came" (McNulty 2019). In fact, all four of the legislators were U.S. citizens, and all were born in the United States except Omar, who arrived legally during childhood as a refugee from Somalia. Trump's statement received widespread condemnation, with critics describing his castigation of people of color as foreign or "other" as a racist trope. Historians also pointed out that the phrase "go back" was a hallmark of nativist discourse that had targeted many groups of newcomers to the United States over the years (Elving 2019).

Some critics claimed that Trump's stance on immigration reflected common themes in white nationalist ideology. He frequently suggested, for instance, that an influx of nonwhite immigrants from Latin America posed a threat to the nation's demographic makeup and cultural unity. "Putting together the President's claims of cultural threat from immigration with his vilification of nonwhite immigrants, these statements suggest support for white nationalist ideas," Jayashri Srikantiah and Shirin Sinnar wrote in the *Stanford Law Review*. "The Administration has issued a dizzying array of policy changes that explicitly target or disproportionately affect noncitizens of color at the same time that President Trump's statements reflect racist intent" (Srikantiah and Sinnar 2019). Critics also noted that Trump failed to publicly repudiate white nationalism following a violent "Unite the Right" rally in Charlottesville, Virginia, in August 2017, in which a right-wing rally attendee killed a counterprotester with his car. Instead of condemning the white supremacists and neo-Nazis who clashed with counterprotesters, Trump implied moral equivalency between those espousing hatred and those expressing opposition to it by saying that there were "very fine people on both sides" (Holan 2019).

According to critics, Trump's denigration of immigrants and tacit approval of white nationalist ideas created a permissive atmosphere for displays of open hostility toward people viewed as foreign. "He gives it voice. He's their megaphone," said Leonard Zeskind, a historian of the white nationalist movement. "Donald Trump, dumping on immigrants all the time, creates an atmosphere where some people interpret that to be an okay sign for violence against immigrants" (Rucker 2019). In some cases, Trump's followers felt emboldened to express or act upon anti-immigrant feelings. For instance, several highly publicized incidents occurred in which white bystanders accosted nonwhite people for speaking Spanish in public. In May 2018, for instance, a white man grew angry when a New York restaurant worker spoke to another customer in Spanish and threatened to call immigration authorities (Lockhart 2018). In August 2019, a white woman confronted a Puerto Rican member of the U.S. Air Force in a coffee shop in Hawaii for speaking Spanish while in uniform, saying it was "distasteful" (Walters 2019). Such incidents reflected Trump's frequent assertion that everyone should speak English in the United States. In a representative tweet, Trump belittled Republican rival Jeb Bush for being bilingual. "Jeb Bush is crazy, who cares that he speaks Mexican, this is America, English!!" he wrote (Vives and Castillo 2019). Meanwhile, surveys showed that the country was home to 40 million Spanish speakers.

Trump increased the intensity of his anti-immigrant message in an effort to galvanize support for Republican candidates in the months leading up to the 2018 midterm elections. At campaign rallies and on social media, he repeatedly warned about the approach of migrant caravans from Central America, calling them an "invasion" of the United States. Trump returned to these themes in his 2020 presidential campaign, highlighting racial and ethnic divisions in what historian Ruth Ben-Ghiat called "a concerted attempt to construct and legitimize an ideology of hatred against nonwhite people and the idea that whites will be replaced by others" (Rucker 2019).

At one rally in Florida, while discussing how to prevent illegal border crossings, Trump asked a crowd of supporters, "How do you stop these people? You can't." When a person in the audience responded, "Shoot them," Trump chuckled while the crowd cheered. Some critics charged that this exchange amounted to inciting violence. "The president has fallen short of calling for overt violence against minorities and immigrants, but unbalanced minds among us may fail to note the distinction," said former FBI counterintelligence expert Frank Figliuzzi. "If a president paints people of color as the enemy, encourages them to be sent back to where they came from, and implies that no humans want to live in certain American cities, he gives license to those who feel compelled to eradicate what Mr. Trump calls an infestation" (Rucker 2019).

In August 2019, a gunman apparently driven by white nationalist sentiments went on a shooting rampage inside a busy Walmart store in the border city of El Paso, Texas, killing 22 people and injuring more than two dozen others. Prior to the mass shooting, the perpetrator posted an anti-immigrant manifesto on an online message board that echoed some of Trump's rhetoric and warned about the "Hispanic invasion of Texas" (Rucker 2019). Authorities classified the attack as a hate crime targeting Latinos, and critics claimed that Trump's words and actions contributed to it. "He doesn't just tolerate it; he encourages it, calling Mexican immigrants rapists and criminals, warning of an invasion at our border, seeking to ban all people of one religion. Folks are responding to this," said then-Democratic presidential candidate Beto O'Rourke, a native of El Paso. "He is saying that some people are inherently defective or dangerous, reminiscent of something that you might hear in the Third Reich, not something that you expect in the United States of America" (Rucker 2019). Republicans argued that the president could not be held responsible for the actions of mentally unbalanced individuals.

Responses to Hostility

For many Latinos, the El Paso massacre underscored the fear and anxiety they felt under the Trump administration. Both citizens and noncitizens of Latino ethnicity reported feeling less safe and more vulnerable to profiling, civil rights violations, and hate crimes. Such feelings of insecurity led many Latinos to alter their daily routines and behavior in an effort to remain "under the radar" and avoid confrontation with immigration agents or Trump supporters. Surveys revealed that many members of the Latino community felt reluctant to report criminal activity, claim public benefits, enroll their children in public schools, and utilize healthcare services (Pierce, Bolter, and Selee 2018). "Hostile policy and rhetoric regarding immigrant families can create a form of structural racism rendering immigrants (particularly those entering illegally) racialized, devalued, dehumanized 'others,' with wider society increasingly normalized to the stereotyping and suffering of this group," wrote researcher Laura Wood. "This in turn impacts the social determinants of health for immigrants via multiple pathways that increase and drive cyclical inequalities in health and well-being. . . . Recent U.S. policy decisions risk further Hispanic isolation, stress, and disengagement with health services, creating substantial health inequalities for immigrant children" (Wood 2018).

In addition to affecting the health and welfare of the Latino community, critics noted that an atmosphere of hostility toward immigrants also had the potential to inflict harm on the larger society. Studies suggested that perceived negative attitudes about foreign-born people had a chilling effect on visa requests for tourism, college enrollment, and employment in the United States. Critics warned that this effect could result in the loss of highly skilled foreign workers, which could make the United States less competitive in a global economy (Pierce, Bolter, and Selee 2018). Critics also pointed out that recent immigrants played a vital role in U.S. military preparedness by serving in the armed forces. By drastically reducing legal immigration, the Trump administration risked losing a valuable source of knowledge about the languages, customs, and inner workings of other nations. Finally, critics charged that harsh anti-immigrant policies and rhetoric harmed the international reputation of the United States and limited the government's ability to advocate for fairness, equality, and human rights on the global stage.

Some Latinos responded to the El Paso shooting and other hostile acts by becoming more politically active in an effort to oppose Trump's immigration policies and counteract anti-immigrant messages. "We have been smeared by political rhetoric and murdered in violent hate crimes," said an open letter signed by more than 200 prominent Latino actors, artists, and authors. "We will not be broken. We will not be silenced. We will continue to denounce any hateful and inhumane treatment of our community. We will demand dignity and justice" (Vives and Castillo 2019). Some Latinos studied to become immigration attorneys or therapists to help people affected by family separation, detention, or deportation. Others worked to dispel stereotypes and improve media representation of the 60 million Latinos living in the United States. "Millions of immigrants through generations have come to this land and, brick by brick, made it a country. Now there's an attack on the very DNA of this country," said actor Wilmer Valderrama, whose family hailed from Colombia and Venezuela. "If you're part of those 60 million, you have a major responsibility to make sure that someone doesn't erase your heritage, the struggle and sacrifice that your great-grandparents or grandparents or parents made" (Vives and Castillo 2019).

Although Trump's hardline stance on immigration resonated with much of his Republican base, some analysts saw evidence that it also produced a political backlash. For instance, surveys found that the president's extreme rhetoric about the migrant caravan in the weeks leading up to the 2018 midterm elections alienated swing voters in some tightly contested districts and contributed to the "blue wave," which saw record numbers of women and minority candidates elected to office and enabled the Democratic Party to gain majority control of the U.S. House of Representatives. Critics pointed out that 32 million people of Hispanic ethnicity would be eligible to vote in the 2020 presidential election, making Latinos the largest minority voting bloc with 13 percent of the electorate. "[Trump's] despicable appeals to racism and xenophobia may well have mobilized his hardcore base, but more importantly, it mobilized a backlash from every other group of voters in the nation," wrote Frank Sharry of the immigrant rights organization America's Voice. "In a showdown between Trump's blood and soil nationalism and the America of *E pluribus unum* [the U.S. national motto, meaning 'Out of many, one'], those of us who believe in a multiracial and multiethnic America turned out and won big" (Sharry 2018).

Further Reading

Editorial Board. 2019. "The Real Meaning of 'Send Her Back.'" *New York Times*, July 18, 2019. https://www.nytimes.com/2019/07/18/opinion/trump -rally-send-her-back.html.

Elving, Ron. 2019. "With Latest Nativist Rhetoric, Trump Takes America Back to Where It Came From." NPR, July 16, 2019. https://www.npr.org/2019/07 /16/742000247/with-latest-nativist-rhetoric-trump-takes-america-back -to-where-it-came-from.

Fritze, John. 2019. "Trump Used Words Like 'Invasion' and 'Killer' to Discuss Immigrants at Rallies 500 Times." *USA Today*, August 8, 2019. https:// www.usatoday.com/story/news/politics/elections/2019/08/08/trump -immigrants-rhetoric-criticized-el-paso-dayton-shootings/1936742001/

Graham, David A. 2018. "Why Trump Can't Understand Immigration from 'Shithole Countries.'" *Atlantic*, January 11, 2018. https://www.theatlantic .com/politics/archive/2018/01/trump-haiti-el-salvador-africa/550358/.

Holan, Angie Drobnic. 2019. "In Context: Donald Trump's 'Very Fine People on Both Sides' Remarks." PolitiFact, April 26, 2019. https://www.politifact.com /truth-o-meter/article/2019/apr/26/context-trumps-very-fine-people -both-sides-remarks/.

Lockhart, P. R. 2018. "A White Lawyer Threatened to Call ICE on Spanish- Speaking Restaurant Workers. Twitter Is Tearing Him Apart." Vox, May 17, 2018. https://www.vox.com/identities/2018/5/16/17362712/white -man-lawyer-threatens-spanish-speaking-workers-new-york-aaron -schlossberg.

McNulty, Matt. 2019. "Meet 'The Squad': The Four Democratic Congresswomen of Color Trump Blasted in Racist Tweets." *People*, July 17, 2019. https:// people.com/politics/meet-aoc-the-squad-ilhan-omar-rashida-tlaib -ayanna-pressley/.

Partelow, Lisette, and Philip E. Wolgin. 2018. "The Trump Administration's Harsh Immigration Policies Are Harming Schoolchildren." Center for American Progress, November 30, 2018. https://www.americanprogress .org/issues/education-k-12/news/2018/11/30/461555/trump-admin istrations-harsh-immigration-policies-harming-schoolchildren/.

Pierce, Sarah, Jessica Bolter, and Andrew Selee. 2018. "U.S. Immigration Policy under Trump: Deep Changes and Lasting Impacts." Migration Policy Institute, July 2018. https://www.migrationpolicy.org/research/us-immi gration-policy-trump-deep-changes-impacts.

Reuters. 2019. "Survey: Trump's Immigration Rhetoric Is Negatively Impacting Latinos' Health." NBC News, November 4, 2019. https://www.nbcnews

.com/news/latino/survey-trump-s-immigration-rhetoric-negatively
-impacting-latinos-health-n1076011.

Rucker, Philip. 2019. "'How Do You Stop These People?' Trump's Anti-Immigrant Rhetoric Looms over El Paso Massacre." *Washington Post*, August 4,
2019. https://www.washingtonpost.com/politics/how-do-you-stop-these
-people-trumps-anti-immigrant-rhetoric-looms-over-el-paso-massacre
/2019/08/04/62d0435a-b6ce-11e9-a091-6a96e67d9cce_story.html.

Sharry, Frank. 2018. "Experts Agree: In 2018 Midterms, Xenophobia Backfired
and Latino Voters Turned Out." America's Voice, November 19, 2018.
https://americasvoice.org/press_releases/experts-agree-in-2018
-midterms-xenophobia-backfired-and-latino-voters-turned-out/.

Srikantiah, Jayashri, and Shirin Sinnar. 2019. "White Nationalism as Immigration Policy." *Stanford Law Review*, March 2019. https://www.stanford
lawreview.org/online/white-nationalism-as-immigration-policy/.

Vives, Ruben, and Andrea Castillo. 2019. "Trump's Policies, as Well as
Anti-Immigrant Violence, Disturbed These Latinos. Now They're Taking
Action." *Los Angeles Times*, October 9, 2019. https://www.latimes.com
/california/story/2019-10-09/trump-immigration-violence-latinos.

Walters, Shamar. 2019. "Air Force Member Called 'Distasteful' for Speaking
Spanish in Uniform." NBC News, August 15, 2019. https://www.nbcnews
.com/news/latino/air-force-member-called-distasteful-speaking-spanish
-uniform-n1042921.

Wood, Laura. 2018. "Impact of Punitive Immigration Policies, Parent-Child
Separation, and Child Detention on the Mental Health and Development
of Children." *BMJ Paediatrics* 2(1): e000338, September 26, 2018.
doi:10.1136/bmjpo-2018-000338.

Global Response to Family Separation and Child Detention

For generations, many people around the world viewed the United
States as a land of freedom and equal opportunity, where anyone willing to
work hard could achieve the "American dream" of prosperity. As a nation
built by immigrants, the United States gained a reputation as a melting pot
society that welcomed newcomers and valued diversity. These ideas made
the United States a leading destination for migrants from around the world
for two centuries. A 2018 Pew Research Center survey found that the U.S.
population included 44.4 million foreign-born individuals. This total represented 18 percent of the world's total migrants—more than the next four
largest destination countries combined—as well as 14 percent of the total
U.S. population (Gonzalez-Barrera and Connor 2019).

For the United States and other destination countries, rapid increases
in the number of people seeking entry posed challenges to immigration

policies and stretched national resources. Although international migration rates remained fairly constant at around 3 percent of the world's population from 1990 to 2017, the total global population increased by 42 percent. As a result, the number of people worldwide living outside of their countries of origin grew from 153 million to 258 million during this 27-year period (UNICEF 2018). People displaced by war, natural disasters, and other means compounded the overall increase in global migration. A record 68.5 million people worldwide fled from war and persecution in 2017, including 25.4 million people deemed refugees— meaning that they were unable to return to their home countries due to a well-founded fear of persecution or violence on the basis of race, religion, nationality, group membership, or political opinion. An unprecedented 52 percent of these refugees were children under age 18 (Prisco 2018a), which reflected an upward trend in child migration during the early twenty-first century. The United Nations High Commissioner for Refugees (UNHCR) reported that the number of children forcibly displaced by violence or insecurity worldwide more than doubled between 2005 and 2015 (Wood 2018).

The growth in international migration and surge in refugees from war-torn regions of Africa and the Middle East put pressure on many destination countries, including Germany, the United Kingdom, France, Canada, Australia, Spain, and Italy. At the same time, the United States also experienced a regional surge of migrants and asylum seekers from Central America, which included a high percentage of families with children and unaccompanied minors. In 2014, during the Barack Obama administration, U.S. immigration authorities apprehended more than 60,000 unaccompanied migrant children attempting to cross the U.S.– Mexico border. The majority were teenagers fleeing from poverty, corruption, gang violence, or domestic abuse in El Salvador, Guatemala, and Honduras. Although the number of unaccompanied migrant children declined to around 10,000 in 2015, it increased steadily from that point onward to exceed 76,000 in 2019, during the Donald Trump administration. That same year saw nearly 474,000 family units apprehended by U.S. Customs and Border Protection (2019). This influx of children and families overwhelmed the personnel and resources available to process, transport, feed, and shelter them.

Migrant Family Separation Draws Criticism

A vocal critic of President Obama's handling of the 2014 immigration crisis, President Trump vowed to make significant changes to U.S. policy to stem the flow of Central American migrants to the United States. For instance, he promised to build a wall along the 1,900-mile length of the U.S.–Mexico border. He also promised to tighten security and increase enforcement measures in the border region. Finally, Trump vowed to end the Obama policy known to critics as "catch and release," which complied with legal restrictions on child detention by releasing entire families from immigration custody pending the resolution of their asylum or deportation hearings. Trump claimed that this lenient policy created incentives for migrant families and unaccompanied minors to enter the country illegally.

In the spring of 2018, Trump administration officials announced the zero tolerance policy, which required immigration authorities to prosecute anyone caught crossing the border illegally, including asylum seekers and families with children. They said the new policy eliminated the catch-and-release loophole and served as a powerful deterrent to prevent Central American families and unaccompanied minors from migrating to the United States. With legal restrictions limiting the amount of time children could be held in detention, however, the zero tolerance policy resulted in the separation of families. While migrant parents and other adult relatives went to detention facilities to await prosecution, migrant children were transferred to shelters for unaccompanied minors operated by the Office of Refugee Resettlement (ORR).

Within a few weeks, Trump's zero tolerance policy caused more than 2,000 migrant children—including infants and toddlers—to be taken away from their adult caregivers and shipped off to distant ORR shelters, often without adequate means of tracking their location or enabling them to communicate with their relatives. In some cases, parents were deported back to their home countries while their children remained in U.S. custody. Trump blamed family separation on Democrats for refusing to reform outdated immigration laws, and he urged migrant parents to avoid separation by not bringing children across the border.

As photographs of sobbing children and anguished parents appeared in newspapers and magazines, and an audiotape of separated children wailing for their mothers went viral online and played on the floor of Congress, the separation of migrant families at the border generated public outrage in the United States. Critics described the policy as cruel, inhumane, and a violation of human rights. "Families are the foundational element of our society and they must be able to stay together," said Cardinal Daniel DiNardo, president of the U.S. Conference of Catholic Bishops. "While protecting our borders is important, we can and must do better as a government, and as a society, to find other ways to ensure that safety. Separating babies from their mothers is not the answer and is immoral" (Prisco 2018b).

The family separation policy also received worldwide condemnation. Although several of Trump's immigration initiatives had generated global opposition—including the Muslim travel ban, the proposed border wall, and steep reductions in refugee admissions—the separation of migrant families brought a new level of international scrutiny to U.S. immigration practices. Dozens of prominent world political and religious leaders spoke out publicly against the policy. Then UK prime minister Theresa May described it as "deeply disturbing" and "not something we agree with," while Canadian prime minister Justin Trudeau said, "What's going on in the United States is wrong. I can't imagine what the families living through this are enduring." Iranian supreme leader Ayatollah Ali Khamenei issued a statement calling family separation a "crime" and accusing the Trump administration of acting with "complete maliciousness" (Ward 2018). Pope Francis told an interviewer that "separating children from their parents goes against natural law" (Bowden 2019).

Some of the most intense global criticism came from representatives of the United Nations (UN). Many UN officials denounced the family separation policy and called upon Trump to rescind it. They noted that children deserved special protection no matter where they were born and that children possessed human rights regardless of their immigration status. "The practice of separating families amounts to arbitrary and unlawful interference in family life, and is a serious violation of the rights of the child," said Ravina Shamdasani, spokesperson for the UN Office of the High Commissioner for Human Rights (OHCHR). "The child's best interest should always come first, including over migration management objectives and other administrative concerns" (McCarthy and Sepehr 2018).

High-ranking UN officials cited medical evidence showing that the trauma of family separation caused severe and lasting harm to children's psychological health and development. "The thought that any state would seek to deter parents by inflicting such abuse on children is unconscionable," said Zeid Ra'ad al-Hussein, who served as the UN High Commissioner for Human Rights through 2018. "There are effective ways to ensure border control without putting families through the lasting psychological trauma of child-parent separation," added UN High Commissioner for Refugees Filippo Grandi. "UNHCR stands ready to support the United States in implementing humane and secure alternatives" (Prisco 2018b).

Several UN representatives noted that family separation violated international human rights agreements, including the Convention on the

Rights of the Child, a 1990 treaty that the United States was the only nation not to ratify. The convention stated that "a child shall not be separated from his or her parents against their will, except when competent authorities subject to judicial review determine, in accordance with applicable law and procedures, that such separation is necessary for the best interests of the child." It also required that "a child who is seeking refugee status or who is considered a refugee in accordance with applicable international or domestic law and procedures shall, whether unaccompanied or accompanied by his or her parents or by any other person, receive appropriate protection and humanitarian assistance" (United Nations 1990).

Migrant Child Detention Encounters Opposition

In the face of intense opposition, Trump issued Executive Order 13841 rescinding the zero tolerance policy on June 20, 2018. A few days later, a federal judge ordered the reunification of migrant families and prohibited further separations except in cases where the parents posed a danger to the children. Critics charged that U.S. immigration officials continued separating families for dubious reasons, such as parents having records of traffic violations or other minor offenses or children crossing the border with adult relatives other than their parents. Separated children and unaccompanied minors were held in immigration detention facilities near the border until they could be transferred to ORR shelters. During fiscal year 2019, the United States held a record 69,550 migrant children in custody, an increase of 42 percent from the previous year (Sherman, Mendoza, and Burke 2019).

Beginning in the spring of 2019, a series of reports raised concerns about conditions in detention facilities operated by federal immigration agencies—especially those that held children. Immigrant rights activists, doctors, progressive lawmakers, journalists, and other observers described frightened, crying children dressed in filthy clothing, confined in overcrowded "cages" made of chain-link fencing, sleeping on concrete floors under Mylar blankets, and lacking access to soap, toothbrushes, and other basic necessities. Seven migrant children died while in the custody of U.S. immigration agencies during Trump's presidency. "As a pediatrician, but also as a mother and a former head of state, I am deeply shocked that children are forced to sleep on the floor in overcrowded facilities, without access to adequate healthcare or food, and with poor sanitation conditions," said Michelle Bachelet, the UN High Commissioner for Human Rights (Graf 2019).

The UN, along with its various agencies, called on the United States and other countries to end child detention worldwide. A 2019 UN progress report on the detention of asylum seekers and refugees said, "The [UNHCR] position is that children should not be detained for immigration-related purposes, irrespective of their legal/migratory status or that of their parents" (Graf 2019). The UN report cited studies showing that detention had long-lasting, harmful effects on children's psychological and physical health, regardless of the duration, the conditions, and the presence or absence of family members. UN representatives asserted that the Trump administration's migrant child detention policies violated the Convention on the Rights of the Child as well as fundamental human rights. "[There is] nothing normal about detaining children," Shamdasani stated. "It is never in the best interests of the child and always constitutes a child rights violation" (McCarthy and Sepehr 2018).

Trump administration officials and supporters pointed out that other countries employed immigration policies and practices that led to the detention of migrant children, whether unaccompanied or with family members. Although data was not widely available, most major destination countries reported far lower numbers of child migrant detainees than the United States. The United Kingdom detained 42 migrant children in 2017, for instance, while Canada detained 155 minors in 2018. Defenders of the U.S. treatment of detainees also noted that such countries as Australia and Greece have struggled to cope with surges of asylum seekers and have faced criticism for detaining migrants in overcrowded or unsanitary conditions. "While few countries can take the moral high ground regarding the detention of children for immigration purposes," wrote researcher Laura Wood, "the systematic separation and detention of immigrant families en masse, without warning or opportunity to challenge, is a phenomenon specific to recent U.S. Trump administration policy" (Wood 2018).

Some critics argued that the Trump administration's harsh immigration policies damaged the United States' international reputation. "This U.S. policy triggers a sense that a distinct red-line is being crossed, a drift to casual inhumanity in the regulation of borders that states and international organizations feel compelled to call out," wrote UN human rights expert Fionnuala Ní Aoláin. "These views on the administration's policies will likely be ignored or derided by the administration itself, but when states succumb to cruel and intolerable policies, there remains a humane global order that will identify and call out the unacceptable and remind us where moral clarity lies" (Ní Aoláin 2018).

UN representatives suggested that member states, including the United States, work together to develop a global approach to handling the large and growing number of refugees worldwide. "We are at a watershed, where success in managing forced displacement globally requires a new and far more comprehensive approach so that countries and communities aren't left dealing with this alone," said Grandi (Prisco 2018a). The UN strategy involved keeping families together whenever possible, protecting children from exploitation and violence, providing access to education and health services, ending the detention of children, and developing humane alternatives to detention. Ireland and Costa Rica eliminated child migrant detention by immediately referring unaccompanied minors to child protection services, for instance, while Malta, Indonesia, and Malaysia implemented case-management systems as a cost-effective alternative to immigration detention (Graf 2019). Other programs worked to address the root causes of migration in countries of origin. In El Salvador, for instance, the nonprofit organization U.S. Committee for Refugees and Immigrants (USCRI) established the Livelihoods project to provide job skills training to young adults who were deported from the United States (Sherman, Mendoza, and Burke 2019).

Further Reading

Bowden, John. 2019. "Pope Francis Says He Would Tell Trump That Family Separations Go 'against Natural Law.'" *The Hill*, May 29, 2019. https://thehill .com/policy/international/445987-pope-francis-says-he-would-tell -trump-separating-children-from-their.

Gonzalez-Barrera, Ana, and Phillip Connor. 2019. "Around the World, More Say Immigrants Are a Strength Than a Burden." Pew Research Center, March 14, 2019. https://www.pewresearch.org/global/2019/03/14/around-the -world-more-say-immigrants-are-a-strength-than-a-burden/.

Graf, Alex. 2019. "UN Calls for End to Migrant Child Detention Worldwide." *Globe Post*, September 16, 2019. https://theglobepost.com/2019/09/16/un -child-migrant-detention/.

McCarthy, Joe, and Jana Sepehr. 2018. "UN Accuses US of Human Rights Violations for Separating Migrant Families." Global Citizen, June 6, 2018. https://www.globalcitizen.org/en/content/un-us-human-rights-abuses -child-migrants/.

Ní Aoláin, Fionnuala. 2018. "Global Response to President Trump's Family Separation via 'Zero Tolerance' Detention Policy." Just Security, June 30, 2018. https://www.justsecurity.org/58783/global-responses-president-trumps -family-separation-zero-tolerance-detention-policy/.

Prisco, Joanna. 2018a. "More Than Half the World's Refugees Are Children." Global Citizen, June 19, 2018. https://www.globalcitizen.org/en/content /un-refugee-agency-global-trends-report-unhcr-stats/.

Prisco, Joanna. 2018b. "World Political and Religious Leaders Condemn US Policy of Separating Migrant Kids." Global Citizen, June 19, 2018. https:// www.globalcitizen.org/en/content/us-migrant-families-policy-world -leaders-condemn/.

Sherman, Christopher, Martha Mendoza, and Garance Burke. 2019. "U.S. Held a Record Number of Migrant Kids in Custody This Year." PBS, November 12, 2019. https://www.pbs.org/wgbh/frontline/article/u-s-held-record-69 -thousand-migrant-children-in-custody-in-2019/

UNICEF. 2018. "Child Migration." December 2018. https://data.unicef.org/topic /child-migration-and-displacement/migration/.

United Nations. 1990. "Convention on the Rights of the Child." Office of the High Commissioner for Human Rights, September 2, 1990. https://www .ohchr.org/EN/ProfessionalInterest/Pages/CRC.aspx/.

U.S. Customs and Border Protection. 2019. "Southwest Border Migration FY 2019." Department of Homeland Security, October 29, 2019. https://www .cbp.gov/newsroom/stats/sw-border-migrationhttps://www.cbp.gov /newsroom/stats/sw-border-migration.

Ward, Alex. 2018. "How the World Is Reacting to Trump's Family Separation Policy." Vox, June 20, 2018. https://www.vox.com/world/2018/6/20 /17483738/trump-family-separation-border-trudeau-may-reaction.

Wood, Laura. 2018. "Impact of Punitive Immigration Policies, Parent-Child Separation, and Child Detention on the Mental Health and Development of Children." *BMJ Paediatrics* 2(1): e000338, September 26, 2018. doi:10.1136/bmjpo-2018-000338.

Alternatives for U.S. Immigration Policy

Immigration has long been one of the most contentious issues in American politics. Successive generations of U.S. leaders have struggled to find fair, just, and compassionate answers to questions involving who should or should not be allowed to enter the United States—as well as who should be forced to leave. A 2017 Gallup survey found that more than 150 million adults worldwide wanted to move to the United States, making it the most desired destination in the world for immigration (Esipova, Pugliese, and Ray 2018). As of 2019, nearly 5 million people waited in immigration backlogs for green cards to become legal permanent residents of the United States and gain a chance to become naturalized citizens. Meanwhile, U.S. Customs and Border Protection (CBP) apprehended more than 850,000 people trying to enter the country illegally at the southern border, and an estimated 11 million foreign-born people lived in the United States without authorization (Golshan 2019). The sheer number of immigrants seeking to enter the United States forced government policymakers to make difficult decisions regarding how many newcomers to admit, how to choose from among the many applicants, how to prevent unauthorized entry, and what to do about undocumented immigrants.

From the time he took office in 2017, President Donald Trump portrayed immigration as a negative force in American society. He enacted many policies that aimed to restrict immigration, such as banning people from Muslim-majority countries and reducing refugee admissions by 60 percent. Trump also imposed measures intended to deter unauthorized immigration, including constructing a wall along the U.S.–Mexico border and increasing arrests and detention of people caught crossing the border illegally. Trump's hardline stance on immigration emerged as a key issue in the 2018 midterm elections and again in the 2020 presidential race. Most Democratic candidates criticized Republican policies and proposed alternative plans for immigration reform that reversed many of the restrictions Trump put in place. They suggested decriminalizing border crossing, expanding refugee admissions, providing a path to citizenship for undocumented immigrants, and abolishing the U.S. Immigration and Customs Enforcement agency (ICE). In general, opponents of Trump's policies portrayed immigration as a positive force in American society and sought to welcome newcomers. "America's elected representatives have a duty to regulate who comes in and when," said former President George W. Bush. "In meeting this responsibility, it helps to remember that America's immigrant history made us who we are. Amid all the complications of policy, may we never forget that immigration is a blessing and a strength" (Trimble 2019).

Border Security and Enforcement

At campaign rallies, Trump frequently characterized immigrants as criminals and terrorists. He also warned about immigrants taking jobs from deserving Americans and using public health and welfare services at taxpayer expense. Critics argued that his anti-immigrant rhetoric stoked fear and bigotry among his supporters. In contrast, Democratic presidential candidates tended to characterize immigrants as ordinary, law-abiding people motivated by the same hopes and dreams that inspired previous generations of newcomers to make the difficult journey to the United States. They claimed that hardworking immigrants played a vital role in the U.S. economy by filling low-paying jobs in factories, farms, hotels, and restaurants that most Americans did not want. Leading Democratic candidates made their opposing views clear by vowing to change virtually all of Trump's immigration policies. "Trump has waged an unrelenting assault on our values and our history as a nation of immigrants," said former vice president Joe Biden. "It's wrong, and it stops when Joe Biden is elected president" (Pramuk 2019). "My first executive orders will be to reverse every single thing President Trump has done to demonize and harm immigrants," added Senator Bernie Sanders (D-CT) (Golshan 2019).

Democratic presidential hopefuls opposed Trump's approach to border security and enforcement, which centered on building a wall along the 1,900-mile border between the United States and Mexico. They argued that the proposed wall was unnecessary, unrealistic, and prohibitively expensive. Some also characterized the wall as racist, claiming that Trump only seemed to care about preventing nonwhite migrants from crossing the southern border from Mexico and never discussed similar measures to prevent white migrants from crossing the 5,500-mile northern border from Canada. Although polls showed that American voters supported border security in general, 60 percent opposed building a wall and felt it would do little to prevent illegal immigration (Newport 2019). Most Democratic candidates released immigration plans that called for halting wall construction and funneling those funds into other immigration reforms.

Led by former San Antonio mayor and U.S. Department of Housing and Urban Development secretary Julián Castro, some Democrats proposed decriminalizing unauthorized border crossing. Castro promoted an immigration plan that called for repealing Title 8, Section 1325 of the U.S. Code, which made it a misdemeanor offense to enter the United States without documentation. Although the law was introduced in 1929, federal prosecutors rarely charged border crossers with the crime of "illegal entry" until the early twenty-first century. Since then, however, immigration offenses often accounted for more than half of all federal prosecutions. Castro blamed Section 1325 for Trump's zero tolerance policy, a controversial enforcement tactic that resulted in the separation of migrant families caught crossing the border together. He also claimed that illegal-entry prosecutions led to prolonged detention of migrants in overcrowded and unsanitary conditions.

By making unauthorized border crossing a civil violation—basically equivalent to a parking ticket—rather than a federal crime, Castro planned to end the inhumane treatment of migrants in the name of immigration enforcement. Although people who entered the country illegally could still be deported, they would no longer be subject to criminal penalties for breaking the law. "Proposing that illegal entry no longer be a federal crime is the policy equivalent of the 'no human is illegal' slogan—a way to combat hawkish attitudes toward the 'rule of law' by challenging the idea that migration ought to be a matter of crime and punishment to begin with," Dara Lind explained for Vox. "But it's also a key justification for reversing the past few decades of border crackdown, by unpinning immigration enforcement—at least when it comes to unauthorized immigrants themselves—from crime" (Lind 2019).

Although several Democratic presidential contenders endorsed Castro's suggestion, others expressed concern that decriminalization might be misconstrued as an "open borders" policy and lead to even larger flows of migrants across the southern border. "This is tantamount to a public declaration (repeated and amplified by smugglers in Central America) that our borders are effectively open to all," warned former Department of Homeland Security secretary Jeh Johnson (Editorial Board 2019). Biden, for instance, rejected decriminalization in his immigration plan, arguing that Democrats risked alienating swing voters by loosening border security.

Most Democrats favored alternatives to detention for immigration enforcement, such as electronic monitoring using ankle tethers and community supervision by social workers. Senator Elizabeth Warren (D-MA) released an immigration plan that proposed reducing migrant detention and eliminating government use of private detention facilities for migrants. She also expressed support for expanding the number of immigration courts, making them independent, and establishing a public defender program to represent the rights of migrants in court. Warren and other Democrats criticized the Trump administration for creating a huge backlog in asylum hearings—with 850,000 cases pending and only 450 judges available to hear them—and keeping asylum seekers in detention for months on end while they awaited action on their requests (Golshan 2019). By speeding up processing and limiting detention of minors, Warren planned to free up CBP resources for other aspects of border enforcement, such as preventing human trafficking and screening cargo for counterfeit goods, illegal drugs, and other contraband.

Many of Trump's policies—including family separation and child detention—aimed to deter Central American migrants from attempting to enter the United States. Opponents claimed that these harsh border enforcement measures did not offer effective or permanent solutions to unauthorized migration. Instead, they argued that U.S. leaders should do more to address the socioeconomic conditions driving people to leave their home countries, such as poverty, gang violence, drug cartels, and political instability. Biden, for instance, proposed investing $4 billion in the Northern Triangle countries of El Salvador, Guatemala, and Honduras to help eliminate violence and corruption and promote economic development (Pramuk 2019).

Legal Immigration

Although Trump expressed a desire to support immigrants who followed the rules, applied for visas, and waited patiently for admission to the United States, many of his policies restricted the number and type of immigrants allowed to become permanent legal residents each year. Trump vowed to cut off two of the main legal channels through which newcomers gained access to U.S. visas: the family-based preference or "chain migration" system and the diversity visa lottery. The family-based preference channel enabled U.S. citizens and green card holders to sponsor close relatives for admission. The diversity visa lottery randomly distributed green cards to 55,000 applicants from countries that sent low numbers of immigrants to the United States over the previous five years. Trump proposed replacing these immigration channels with "Build America" visas awarded on a merit-based point system. Trump's system favored people who were young, well educated, and possessed valuable skills. Successful applicants also had to demonstrate financial self-sufficiency, English proficiency, and basic knowledge of U.S. government and history.

Critics of the Trump plan noted that it represented a dramatic shift in the criteria used to select which potential immigrants received green cards to live and work in the United States. In comparison to 2017, it would increase the percentage of people who gained legal permanent resident status through economic or employment-based categories from 12 percent to 57 percent. Meanwhile, it would decrease the percentage of immigrants who received visas through family sponsorship from 66 percent to 33 percent. Trump's proposal would also eliminate diversity visas, which accounted for 5 percent of new immigrants in 2017 (Chishti and Bolter 2019). Critics of Trump's plan argued that family reunification and ethnic diversity were important priorities that should remain part of U.S. immigration policy. They also noted that implementing the proposed change in selection criteria would effectively throw out 4 million family-based visa applications and force those people—some of whom had been waiting in line for many years—to reapply under the new merit-based point system (Anderson 2019). "The bottom line is that we need wider legal immigration channels," said Douglas Rivlin of the liberal immigration reform group America's Voice, "but do you move the people who have been waiting in line first and then establish wider channels?" (Golshan 2019).

Finally, some Democrats contended that Trump's merit-based plan favored wealthy and well-educated foreigners as part of a broader Republican effort to shift the demographic makeup of new immigrants away from Central America and Africa and toward Asia and Europe.

Trump also dramatically lowered the annual cap on refugee admissions, to an all-time low of 18,000 for 2020, and asserted that fraudulent claims fueled the massive increases in Central American migrants seeking asylum in the United States. "Our nation has a proud history of affording protection to those fleeing government persecutions," Trump stated. "Unfortunately, legitimate asylum seekers are being displaced by those lodging frivolous claims" (Hermani 2019). Democratic presidential candidates rejected Trump's arguments about refugees and asylum seekers. Warren promised to raise the annual cap on admissions to 125,000 within one year of taking office and to 175,000 for the remainder of her term. She also pledged to revoke Trump's "stay in Mexico" policy, which forced Central American asylum seekers to remain in dangerous Mexican border towns while U.S. officials processed their requests, and to enact measures to ensure that asylees received due process in immigration court hearings.

Undocumented Immigrants

An integral part of the immigration debate focused on what to do about the estimated 11 million people living in the United States without legal status. This total included approximately 700,000 recipients of Deferred Action for Childhood Arrivals (DACA), an Obama-era program that extended temporary protection from deportation to immigrants brought to the United States as children prior to June 2007. It also included around 300,000 recipients of Temporary Protected Status (TPS) from deportation on a humanitarian basis. Trump opposed any sort of amnesty program that would confer legal status on undocumented immigrants, arguing that they should not benefit from breaking the law by entering the country without authorization. "No one will be immune and exempt from enforcement," he told a crowd of supporters at a campaign rally. "Anyone who has entered the United States illegally is subject to deportation. That is what it means to have laws and a country" (Berenson and Miller 2016). He asserted that the only way for undocumented people to attain legal status was to leave the country and then return through proper immigration channels.

Trump occasionally expressed support for mass deportation of all undocumented immigrants. He authorized ICE to conduct investigations and raids aimed at rounding up and deporting people without legal status. Although he attempted to remove protections from DACA recipients, known as Dreamers, a federal court blocked his initial efforts. Trump also threatened to withhold funding from so-called sanctuary cities that refused to use their municipal resources to assist federal authorities in enforcing immigration law. Critics derided Trump's determination to deport all undocumented people as cruel, unrealistic, and a waste of law enforcement resources. They pointed out that the majority of undocumented people had resided in the United States for a decade or more and had established homes, families, businesses, and community ties. They also noted that ICE raids generated fear and anxiety in immigrant communities, causing residents to avoid reporting crimes, seeking medical treatment, or utilizing public assistance programs. In addition, critics charged that deportation often separated families and created hardships for children.

All of the major Democratic presidential candidates proposed creating a path to citizenship for undocumented people. Most proposals required immigrants to meet some conditions in order to gain legal status, such as learning English, passing a criminal background check, holding a job, and paying taxes. A 2019 Gallup poll found strong voter support for this approach, with 81 percent of respondents indicating that they approved a pathway to citizenship (Newport 2019). Democratic candidates also favored establishing permanent protections for DACA recipients, whether through legislative or executive action. Some also suggested expanding the program to include parents of the Dreamers.

Some progressive Democrats expressed support for the movement to abolish ICE. Proponents pointed out that the agency had been established in response to the terrorist attacks against the United States on September 11, 2001, as part of the Department of Homeland Security (DHS). As a result, according to critics, ICE agents tended to view immigrants and people of color with suspicion and treat them as potential threats to national security. Although the leading presidential candidates stopped short of endorsing this position, some proposed limiting ICE's power. Warren, for instance, suggested creating zones where people could be safe from immigration enforcement in schools, courthouses, and hospitals.

Critics of the immigration plans proposed by Democratic frontrunners argued that the candidates failed to develop comprehensive approaches to immigration reform and instead focused on reversing Trump's controversial policies. "Being opposed to detaining children in cages is easy. Denouncing Trump's xenophobic rhetoric is uncontroversial. So is calling Trump's travel ban against Muslim-majority countries discriminatory,"

Tara Golshan wrote for Vox. "Democratic candidates are, so far, finding those options preferable to working out the details of a comprehensive immigration plan" (Golshan 2019). Others acknowledged that immigration reform, with its many complex decisions and painful compromises, had eluded lawmakers for decades. As a *New York Times* editorial put it, "Some people will get in, others will be kept out, still others will be compelled to leave. Any meaningful effort to reform the country's degrading approach to migrants will fall apart if it pretends a president can simply ignore such choices" (Editorial Board 2019).

Further Reading

Anderson, Stuart. 2019. "Trump Immigration Plan May Throw 4 Million People Off Immigrant Waiting Lists." *Forbes*, May 16, 2019. https://www.forbes.com/sites/stuartanderson/2019/05/16/trump-immigration-plan-may-throw-4-million-people-off-immigrant-waiting-lists/#15cbd3026943.

Berenson, Tessa, and Zeke J. Miller. 2016. "Donald Trump Pivots Back to Hardline Immigration Stance." *Time*, September 1, 2016. https://time.com/4475417/donald-trump-immigration-policy-mexico-deportation/.

Chishti, Muzaffar, and Jessica Bolter. 2019. "'Merit-Based' Immigration: Trump Proposal Would Dramatically Revamp Immigrant Selection Criteria, but with Modest Effects on Numbers." Migration Policy Institute, May 30, 2019. https://www.migrationpolicy.org/article/merit-based-immigration-trump-proposal-immigrant-selection.

Editorial Board. 2019. "All Presidents Are Deporters in Chief." *New York Times*, July 13, 2019. https://www.nytimes.com/2019/07/13/opinion/sunday/trump-deportations-immigration.html.

Esipova, Neli, Anita Pugliese, and Julie Ray. 2018. "More Than 750 Million Worldwide Would Migrate If They Could." Gallup, December 10, 2018. https://news.gallup.com/poll/245255/750-million-worldwide-migrate.aspx.

Golshan, Tara. 2019. "The 2020 Democratic Immigration Debate, Explained." Vox, July 29, 2019. https://www.vox.com/2019/7/29/6741801/2020-democrat-presidential-immigration-debate.

Hermani, Jordyn. 2019. "Trump Pitches His 'Merit-Based' Immigration Proposal." *Politico*, May 16, 2019. https://www.politico.com/story/2019/05/16/trump-merit-based-immigration-policy-1329380.

Lind, Dara. 2019. "Why Julián Castro Started a Democratic Debate Fight over Repealing 'Section 1325.'" Vox, June 26, 2019. https://www.vox.com/2019/6/26/18760665/1325-immigration-castro-democratic-debate.

Newport, Frank. 2019. "Immigration, Public Opinion, and Congress." Gallup, February 12, 2019. https://news.gallup.com/opinion/polling-matters/246665/immigration-public-opinion-congress.aspx.

Pramuk, Jacob. 2019. "Joe Biden Acknowledges 'Pain' Caused by Obama Depor-
    tations as He Unveils Immigration Plan." CNBC, December 11, 2019.
    https://www.cnbc.com/2019/12/11/joe-biden-releases-immigration
    -reform-plan-targeting-trump-border-policies.html.
Trimble, Megan. 2019. "Bush: Immigration Is a Blessing and a Strength." *U.S.
    News and World Report*, March 18, 2019. https://www.usnews.com/news
    /national-news/articles/2019-03-18/george-w-bush-says-immigration-is
    -a-blessing-and-a-strength-at-naturalization-ceremony.

CHAPTER FOUR

Profiles

This chapter provides illuminating biographical profiles of important figures in the development and implementation of the Trump administration's immigration policies, including special policy adviser Stephen Miller and Department of Homeland Security Secretary Kirstjen Nielsen, as well as leading voices of opposition to migrant family separation and migrant child detention, including U.S. Representative Alexandria Ocasio-Cortez and pediatrician Dolly Lucio Sevier.

Stephen Miller (1985–)

White House policy adviser who engineered Trump's migrant family separation policy

Stephen Miller was born on August 23, 1985, in Santa Monica, California. His father, Michael D. Miller, owned a real estate investment company, Cordary Inc., that managed several large rental housing communities. His mother, Miriam Glosser Miller, hailed from a Jewish family that fled ethnic violence in Belarus in the early twentieth century, settled in Pennsylvania, and gained prominence in the retail industry. Although his parents considered themselves liberal Democrats during his youth, Miller developed conservative political views in his early teens after reading *Guns, Crime, and Freedom*, a 1994 book by National Rifle Association president Wayne LaPierre. The book presents gun ownership as a form of personal freedom and attacks gun control and many other progressive ideas as threats to American values.

As an outspoken conservative, Miller often came into conflict with fellow students and teachers at Santa Monica High School, which featured a liberal, multicultural learning environment. Miller wrote articles for the student newspaper, local publications, and conservative blogs in which he expressed hostility toward Hispanic students, who made up 30 percent of the student body. He complained about a school-wide celebration of the Mexican holiday Cinco de Mayo, for instance, and argued that minority students should be required to speak English. "When I entered Santa Monica High School in ninth grade, I noticed a number of students lacked basic English skills," Miller wrote. "Even so, pursuant to district policy, all announcements are written in both Spanish and English. By providing a crutch now, we are preventing Spanish speakers from standing on their own. . . . As politically correct as this may be, it demeans the immigrant population as incompetent, and makes a mockery of the American ideal of personal accomplishment" (Peinado 2017).

Fellow students remembered Miller as intelligent and focused, yet also angry, argumentative, and vehement in defending his ultranationalist views. "He believes multiculturalism is a weakness, that when we celebrate our differences we are ignoring our 'American culture,'" said Nick Silverman, a high school classmate. "He didn't like someone from El Salvador celebrating their homeland, or someone from Vietnam bringing in food from their country of origin. He wanted everyone to celebrate one culture. One country" (Cohan 2017). Upon graduating from high school in 2003, Miller used a quote from former president Theodore Roosevelt in his senior yearbook: "There can be no fifty-fifty Americanism in this country. There is room here for only 100 percent Americanism, only for those who are Americans and nothing else" (Peinado 2017).

Miller went on to attend Duke University in Durham, North Carolina, where he became active in conservative student organizations and associated with such controversial right-wing personalities as anti-immigration activist David Horowitz and white nationalist Richard Spencer. Miller gained national media attention in 2006, when he emerged as a vocal defender of three white Duke men's lacrosse players who were accused of raping a black woman they had hired as a stripper. Miller argued that Duke students and faculty rushed to judgment and condemned the players based on racial identity politics. He celebrated when authorities dropped the charges against the players. "The thing that I'm proudest of is that I spoke out early and often on behalf of American legal principles in the Duke lacrosse case when it was not popular," Miller stated (Wiedeman 2017).

After earning his bachelor's degree in political science in 2007, Miller parlayed his media experience into jobs as a press secretary for Representatives Michele Bachmann (R-MN) and John Shadegg (R-AZ). In 2009, he joined the staff of Senator Jeff Sessions (R-AL), eventually attaining the position of communications director. Miller played an influential role in shaping Sessions' stance on immigration. In 2013, for instance, he wrote speeches that helped the senator defeat a bipartisan immigration reform bill that proposed a path to citizenship for millions of undocumented people. In 2016, Miller became a senior policy adviser for Republican candidate Donald Trump's presidential campaign. He often took the stage at campaign rallies to warm up the crowd prior to Trump's appearance. "Frankly, what makes a warm-up speech work is that my enthusiasm and their enthusiasm are equal," Miller explained. "All of us feel at this juncture in history the potential of a fundamental change. It's a feeling of excitement that comes from knowing that you're part of something really special" (Ioffe 2016).

After Trump prevailed in the November election, Miller served as national policy director for Trump's transition team and then joined the Trump administration as a senior adviser for policy. He quickly turned his focus to immigration policy, working with Sessions and other officials to implement a series of executive orders issued by the new president. Executive Order 13769, for instance, established a "travel ban" that temporarily halted immigration and restricted travel to the United States by citizens of seven predominantly Muslim nations (Iran, Iraq, Libya, Somalia, Sudan, Syria, and Yemen). Administration officials claimed that the controversial measure was necessary to prevent potential terrorists from entering the country. After a federal judge blocked the travel ban, arguing that the administration had failed to provide evidence showing that it would prevent terrorism, Miller denounced the decision in a series of media appearances. "We have a judiciary that has taken far too much power and become in many cases a supreme branch of government," Miller declared. "Our opponents, the media, and the whole world will soon see as we begin to take further actions, that the powers of the president to protect our country are very substantial and will not be questioned" (Cohan 2017). Legal experts criticized his statement, noting that the U.S. Constitution provides for judicial review of executive actions as part of the separation of powers between different branches of government.

Miller played an influential role in shaping other aspects of Trump's immigration policy and messaging. He spoke out in favor of building a wall along the 1,900-mile southern border of the United States to prevent migrants from Mexico and Central America from entering the country illegally. He also supported efforts to force undocumented immigrants to leave the United States, including ending the Deferred Action for

Childhood Arrivals (DACA) program and stepping up raids and deportations by the Immigration and Customs Enforcement (ICE) agency. In the fall of 2017, Miller oversaw the process of determining the annual cap on the number of refugees admitted into the United States. He overcame objections from other officials to set the cap at 45,000 for 2018, a record low and less than half the total allowed by President Barack Obama the previous year. Critics contended that Miller ignored, suppressed, or manipulated data that did not support his plan to reduce the cap, such as a Department of Health and Human Services study suggesting that refugees had a positive economic impact that exceeded the cost of resettlement by $63 billion. "He basically just had a political agenda," one White House official claimed, "to limit the number of foreign nationals who come into our country" (Blitzer 2017). Miller went on to reduce the refugee cap further, to 30,000 for 2019 and to 18,000 for 2020.

Miller also served as the main architect of the Trump administration's "zero tolerance" policy, enacted in spring 2018 in response to statistics showing an increase in migrants—especially families and unaccompanied minors—crossing the border illegally. This policy required U.S. Customs and Border Protection (CBP) officials to arrest and prosecute anyone caught crossing the border illegally, including migrants who claimed to be seeking asylum from a credible fear of persecution and violence in their home countries. Miller argued that the new policy closed a loophole that had previously allowed such individuals to remain in the United States until their asylum applications could be processed. "No nation can have the policy that whole classes of people are immune from immigration law or enforcement," he explained. "It was a simple decision by the administration to have a zero tolerance policy for illegal entry, period. The message is that no one is exempt from immigration law" (Davis and Shear 2018).

Since U.S. law prohibits minor children from being held in criminal detention facilities meant for adults, the zero tolerance policy effectively required immigration officials to separate families that crossed the border together. By mid-June, 2,000 migrant children had been separated from "alleged adult parents" who were caught bringing them across the border illegally (Radnofsky, Andrews, and Fassihi 2018). These children were transferred to shelters operated by the Office of Refugee Resettlement or placed in foster care. Reports soon emerged of traumatized children being held in crowded and unsanitary conditions without adequate supervision or access to basic necessities. In addition, federal agencies failed to track the whereabouts of some children so they could be reunited with family members. In some instances, parents were deported without being able to locate or reclaim their children, who remained in the United States.

As its effects became clear, the Trump administration's family separation policy came under intense criticism. "This is not a zero tolerance policy, this is a zero humanity policy, and we can't let it go on," said Senator Jeff Merkley (D-OR). "Ripping children out of their parents' arms to inflict harm on the child to influence the parents is unacceptable" (Davis and Shear 2018). In the face of public outrage, Trump signed an executive order rescinding the family separation policy on June 20. The controversy continued over the next few months, however, as various federal agencies struggled to reunite migrant children with their families.

Despite the backlash, Miller continued working behind the scenes to promote anti-immigration policies in the Trump administration. In early 2019, he reportedly played a role in securing the resignation of Department of Homeland Security Secretary Kirstjen Nielsen, arguing that the administration needed to adopt a tougher stance to secure the nation's borders. Although Miller's uncompromising approach won favor with Trump and other immigration hardliners, political opponents complained that it presented a major obstacle to bipartisan cooperation on immigration reform. As Senator Dick Durbin (D-IL) stated, "Any effort to kill immigration reform usually has Mr. Miller's fingerprints on it" (Tatum 2018). In the fall of 2019, civil rights groups obtained copies of emails that Miller sent to the conservative website Breitbart News in which he promoted white nationalist ideology. The public release of the emails prompted more than 100 Democratic members of Congress to sign a letter demanding Miller's resignation. "A documented white nationalist has no place in any administration, and especially not in such an influential position," the letter stated (Gamboa 2019).

Further Reading

Blitzer, Jonathan. 2017. "How Stephen Miller Single-Handedly Got the U.S. to Accept Fewer Refugees." *New Yorker*, October 13, 2017. https://www .newyorker.com/news/news-desk/how-stephen-miller-single-handedly -got-the-us-to-accept-fewer-refugees.

Cohan, William D. 2017. "How Stephen Miller Rode White Rage from Duke's Campus to Trump's West Wing." *Vanity Fair*, May 30, 2017. https://www .vanityfair.com/news/2017/05/stephen-miller-duke-donald-trump.

Davis, Julie Hirschfeld, and Michael D. Shear. 2018. "How Trump Came to Enforce a Practice of Separating Migrant Families." *New York Times*, June 16, 2018. https://www.nytimes.com/2018/06/16/us/politics/family -separation-trump.html.

Gamboa, Suzanne. 2019. "After Stephen Miller's White Nationalist Views Outed, Latinos Ask, 'Where's the GOP Outrage?'" NBC News, December 7, 2019.

https://www.nbcnews.com/news/latino/after-stephen-miller-s-white
-nationalist-views-outed-latinos-ask-n1096071.

Ioffe, Julia. 2016. "The Believer." *Politico*, June 27, 2016. https://www.politico.com
/magazine/story/2016/06/stephen-miller-donald-trump-2016-policy
-adviser-jeff-sessions-213992.

Peinado, Fernando. 2017. "How White House Advisor Stephen Miller Went from
Pestering Hispanic Students to Designing Trump's Immigration Policy."
Univision News, February 9, 2017. https://www.univision.com/univision
-news/politics/how-white-house-advisor-stephen-miller-went-from
-pestering-hispanic-students-to-designing-trumps-immigration-policy.

Radnofsky, Louise, Natalie Andrews, and Farnaz Fassihi. 2018. "Trump Administration Defends Family-Separation Policy." *Wall Street Journal*, June 18,
2018. https://www.wsj.com/articles/trump-administration-defends-family
-separation-policy-1529341079.

Tatum, Sophie. 2018. "How Stephen Miller, the Architect behind Trump's Immigration Policies, Rose to Power." CNN, June 23, 2018. https://edition.cnn
.com/2018/06/23/politics/stephen-miller-immigration-family-separation
/index.html.

Wiedeman, Reeves. 2017. "The Duke Lacrosse Scandal and the Birth of the Alt-
Right." *New York Magazine*, April 14, 2017. http://nymag.com/intelligencer
/2017/04/the-duke-lacrosse-scandal-and-the-birth-of-the-alt-right.html.

Kirstjen Nielsen (1972–)

*Homeland Security secretary who implemented the migrant family separation
policy*

Kirstjen Michele Nielsen was born on May 14, 1972, in Colorado
Springs, Colorado. She was the oldest of three children born to James
McHenry Nielsen and Phyllis Michele Nielsen, who both served in the
U.S. Army as medical doctors. During Kirstjen's childhood, the family
relocated to Tampa, Florida, where she attended the private Berkeley Pre-
paratory School. Nielsen went on to earn a bachelor's degree from George-
town University's School of Foreign Service. After working on Capitol Hill
in the office of Senator Connie Mack (R-FL) for two years, Nielsen continued her education at the University of Virginia law school, earning her JD
degree in 1999.

Nielsen practiced corporate law for two years before returning to government service in 2002. She joined the George W. Bush administration in
the wake of the terrorist attacks of September 11, 2001, and contributed to
its efforts to update and strengthen the nation's security policies and infrastructure. As an assistant administrator in the Transportation Security

Administration (TSA), Nielsen helped establish the office of legislative policy and government affairs. She also helped draft new passenger-screening rules for airport security, including the TSA rule limiting carry-on liquids to three-ounce containers stored in clear plastic bags.

During her years in the Bush administration, Nielsen also served as senior director for prevention, preparedness, and response (PPR) in the Homeland Security Council, which later became the Department of Homeland Security (DHS). In this position, she came under criticism for her role in the federal government's slow, ineffective response to Hurricane Katrina, which flooded the city of New Orleans and killed nearly 2,000 people in 2005. Afterward, Nielsen wrote a report outlining the lessons learned from Katrina and suggesting changes to improve disaster response in the future.

In 2007, Nielsen returned to the private sector as general counsel and head of the homeland security division for the Civitas Group, a political strategy, consulting, and lobbying firm. Five years later, a change in ownership led to the dismissal of Nielsen and other top Civitas executives. She then launched her own business, Sunesis Consulting, focusing on cybersecurity issues. Nielsen also served as a senior fellow at George Washington University's Center for Cyber and Homeland Security. In this capacity, she produced risk reports for the World Economic Forum, a nonprofit organization that hosts an annual global summit in Davos, Switzerland. In a 2016 report on the worldwide refugee crisis, Nielsen recommended emphasizing the positive social and economic contributions refugee settlement offered to host countries.

In January 2017, Nielsen accepted a position as chief of staff to DHS Secretary John F. Kelly in the incoming administration of Republican President Donald Trump. Six months later, when Kelly left DHS for the White House to become Trump's chief of staff, Nielsen followed to serve as principal deputy chief of staff. Trump cut her time at the White House short, however, by nominating Nielsen to become the new secretary of DHS. Several conservative media outlets and right-wing pundits criticized the choice, arguing that Nielsen's work with the World Economic Forum suggested that she held pro-immigration views in conflict with Trump's hardline policies. Commentator Ann Coulter described Nielsen as an "open borders zealot," for instance, while Breitbart News called her a "pro-amnesty, Bush bureaucrat" (Guinto 2018).

Other critics asserted that Nielsen lacked the necessary qualifications and experience to oversee a federal agency with $40 billion budget and 240,000 employees. They pointed out that her entire career in government service amounted to less than a decade, and that she had never held a managerial position with more than 15 direct reports. Kelly and other colleagues expressed strong support for Nielsen, however, praising her intelligence, command of the issues, intense focus, and direct, no-nonsense demeanor. The Senate voted 62–37 to confirm her nomination on December 5, 2017, and she took the oath of office the following day.

As the sixth secretary of DHS, Nielsen directed the branch of the U.S. government charged with securing the nation against all manner of threats it might face. DHS handles counterterrorism efforts, disaster preparedness and emergency response, cybersecurity, and protection of critical infrastructure. It also oversees the security of U.S. borders, including overland, maritime, and aviation approaches. As part of its border-security mission, DHS plays an important role in enforcing immigration laws and policies. The DHS agencies involved in immigration investigations and enforcement include the U.S. Immigration and Customs Enforcement (ICE) and U.S. Customs and Border Protection (CBP).

Nielsen generated controversy from the beginning of her tenure by appearing to ignore or downplay issues that many Americans viewed as emerging threats to homeland security. In a May 2018 congressional hearing, for instance, she said she had not reviewed U.S. intelligence assessments indicating that Russia attempted to interfere in the 2016 presidential election. Two months later, Nielsen acknowledged Russia's efforts to influence the election but contradicted the intelligence community's conclusions by claiming Russia's intent was to "cause chaos on both sides" rather than to help Trump win (Goodkind 2018).

Critics also charged that Nielsen did not do enough to stem a rising tide of white supremacist violence in the United States, such as the deadly clash that occurred at an August 2017 Unite the Right rally in Charlottesville, Virginia. When asked about Trump's response to that event— which received widespread criticism for implying moral equivalence between neo-Nazi marchers and counterprotesters—Nielsen echoed the president's controversial comments by saying, "It is not that one side is right, one side is wrong. Anybody that is advocating violence, we need to work to mitigate" (Goodkind 2018).

Immigration quickly emerged as a key issue for Nielsen. Her job as DHS secretary put her in charge of implementing the Trump administration's aggressive policies aimed at securing the southern border of the United States and preventing migrants from entering the country illegally. She took office at the beginning of the longest federal government shutdown in history, which arose mainly due to a dispute between the president and Congress over funding to build a wall along the 1,900-mile U.S.–Mexico border. Although Trump eventually signed an appropriations bill that restored government operations without including wall funding, he continued seeking means to deter migration and pressure Congress to pass tougher anti-immigration laws. At a cabinet meeting in early May, Trump reportedly expressed displeasure with Nielsen's performance and demanded that she make immigration her top priority. "The president is rightly frustrated that existing loopholes and the lack of congressional action have prevented this administration from fully securing the border," she said in a statement released afterward (Guinto 2018).

In response to statistics showing an increase in migrants—especially families and unaccompanied minors—crossing the border illegally, the Trump administration enacted a "zero tolerance" policy in spring 2018. This policy required DHS to treat every illegal border crossing as a criminal offense, put the accused individuals in jail, and refer them to the Department of Justice for prosecution. The policy applied to everyone, including migrants who claimed to be seeking asylum from a credible fear of persecution and violence in their home countries. "Our policy is if you break the law, we will prosecute you," Nielsen explained. "You have an option to go to a port of entry and not illegally cross into our country" (Kopan 2018a).

Since U.S. law prohibited minor children from being held in criminal detention facilities meant for adults, the new policy effectively required DHS to separate families that crossed the border together. Before it took effect, DHS often declined to prosecute adults accompanied by children in order to avoid separating families. Nielsen asserted that adult migrants fraudulently brought unrelated children across the border to exploit this loophole. She claimed that the zero tolerance policy helped protect migrant children from being used and endangered by criminals seeking to enter the United States. "When we separate, we separate because the law tells us to, and that is in the interest of the child," she stated. "Unfortunately, we have seen instances where traffickers have used children to cross the border and gain access illegally" (Kopan 2018b).

By mid-June, DHS had separated 2,000 migrant children from "alleged adult parents" who were caught bringing them across the border illegally (Radnofsky, Andrews, and Fassihi 2018). Since U.S. laws and court rulings limited the amount of time unaccompanied minors could be held in government custody, the migrant children were transferred to shelters operated by the Office of Refugee Resettlement or placed in foster care. Reports soon emerged of traumatized children being held in crowded and unsanitary conditions without adequate supervision or access to basic necessities. In addition, federal agencies failed to track the whereabouts of some children so they could be reunited with family members. In some instances, parents were deported without being able to locate or reclaim their children, who remained in the United States.

As its effects became clear, the Trump administration's family separation policy came under intense criticism. "This is just absolutely unacceptable," said Representative Will Hurd (R-TX). "Taking kids from their mothers is not preventing terrorists or drugs from coming into this country. And so why we would even think that this is a tool that is needed to defend our borders is insane to me." Senator John McCain (R-AZ) called the policy "an affront to the decency of the American people, and contrary to principles and values upon which our nation was founded." In an editorial for the *Washington Post*, former first lady Laura Bush added, "This zero-tolerance policy is cruel. It is immoral. And it breaks my heart" (Chappell and Taylor 2018).

On June 18, Nielsen appeared at White House press conference to defend the controversial policy. Critics charged that she made contradictory and false statements. Nielsen initially denied that the family separation policy existed. Instead, she claimed that the Trump administration was merely enforcing laws put in place by previous administrations. "We do not have a policy of separating families at the border. Period," Nielsen stated. "What has changed is that we no longer exempt entire classes of people who break the law. Everyone is subject to prosecution" (Rizzo 2018). Nielsen blamed Democrats for the resulting humanitarian crisis and demanded that Congress pass legislation to rectify the situation. Republicans controlled both houses of Congress at that time, however, and refused to consider bills that did not include funding for Trump's border wall. Nielsen later admitted that the zero tolerance policy caused the separation of migrant families, but she denied that DHS pursued family separation as a means of deterring illegal border crossings, even as other administration officials characterized deterrence as its main purpose. Following her press conference, *Washington Post* fact-checkers declared that "the doublespeak coming from Trump and top administration officials on this issue is breathtaking" (Rizzo 2018).

Despite repeatedly insisting that he lacked the power to do so, Trump signed an executive order rescinding the family separation policy on June 20. The controversy continued over the next few months, however, as various federal agencies struggled to reunite migrant children with their families. Nielsen came under criticism again in November 2018, when CBP agents fired tear gas into a crowd of Central American migrants attempting to cross the California-Mexico border. Although observers noted that the group included women and small children, Nielsen characterized the migrants as violent criminals who threw rocks at law enforcement personnel.

In December, the deaths of two young migrant children while in custody of CBP brought Nielsen's leadership under renewed scrutiny. Although Nielsen called the deaths "deeply concerning and heartbreaking" and promised to increase medical screenings of migrant children at the border, she also blamed "an immigration system that rewards parents for sending their children across the border alone, a system that prevents parents who bring their children on a dangerous and illegal journey from facing consequences for their actions" (Nielsen 2018).

Several prominent lawmakers responded to the ongoing problems at DHS by calling for Nielsen's resignation. "Under her watch, our government has committed human rights abuses by breaking up families along the southern border," said Senator Kamala Harris (D-CA). "And she has failed to be accountable to and transparent with the American people" (Chappell and Taylor 2018). In April 2019, Trump signaled his displeasure with Nielsen's performance by proclaiming his desire to get tougher on immigration. She responded by submitting her resignation on April 7. Later that day, Trump announced that CBP commissioner Kevin McAleenan would assume the role of acting secretary of DHS. Some of Nielsen's former colleagues argued that she had no choice but to enforce Trump's controversial immigration policies. "She either loses this spectacular job, or she does the bidding of a president who is using these kids in a game of brinkmanship so he can get his wall," said one DHS employee (Guinto 2018).

Further Reading

Chappell, Bill, and Jessica Taylor. 2018. "Defiant Homeland Security Secretary Defends Family Separations." NPR, June 18, 2018. https://www.npr.org/2018/06/18/620972542/we-do-not-have-a-policy-of-separating-families-dhs-secretary-nielsen-says.

Goodkind, Nicole. 2018. "Kirstjen Nielsen Blames Both Sides for Deadly Charlottesville Violence, Claims Russia Didn't Try to Help Trump." *Newsweek*, July 19, 2018. https://www.newsweek.com/kirstjen-nielsen-charlottesville-russia-trump-1033252.

Guinto, Joseph. 2018. "That's Not the Kirstjen We Know." *Politico*, July 2, 2018. https://www.politico.com/magazine/story/2018/07/02/kirstjen-nielsen-immigration-crisis-former-colleagues-218939.

Kopan, Tal. 2018a. "DHS Secretary Defends Separating Families at the Border." CNN, May 15, 2018. https://www.cnn.com/2018/05/15/politics/dhs-separating-families-secretary-nielsen-hearing/index.html.

Kopan, Tal. 2018b. "New DHS Policy Could Separate Families Caught Crossing the Border Illegally." CNN, May 7, 2018. https://www.cnn.com/2018/05/07 /politics/illegal-immigration-border-prosecutions-families-separated /index.html.

Nielsen, Kristjen M. 2018. "Secretary Kristjen M. Nielsen Statement on Passing of Eight-Year-Old Guatemalan Child." U.S. Department of Homeland Security, December 26, 2018. https://www.dhs.gov/news/2018/12/26 /secretary-kirstjen-m-nielsen-statement-passing-eight-year-old -guatemalan-child.

Radnofsky, Louise, Natalie Andrews, and Farnaz Fassihi. 2018. "Trump Administration Defends Family-Separation Policy." *Wall Street Journal*, June 18, 2018. https://www.wsj.com/articles/trump-administration-defends-family -separation-policy-1529341079.

Rizzo, Salvador. 2018. "The Facts about Trump's Policy of Separating Families at the Border." *Washington Post*, June 19, 2018. https://www.washingtonpost .com/news/fact-checker/wp/2018/06/19/the-facts-about-trumps-policy -of-separating-families-at-the-border/.

Alexandria Ocasio-Cortez (1989–)

New York congresswoman who helped expose migrant detention conditions

Alexandria Ocasio-Cortez was born on October 13, 1989, in the Bronx borough of New York City. Her father, Sergio, owned a small architecture firm that offered remodeling and landscaping services. Her mother, Blanca, worked as a housekeeper, school bus driver, and secretary. Ocasio-Cortez spent her early childhood in the diverse Parkchester housing complex surrounded by a large, working-class family with Puerto Rican roots. When she was ready to start school, her parents sought to improve her educational options by purchasing a modest house in Yorktown Heights, an affluent, mostly white suburb located 40 minutes north in Westchester County. Ocasio-Cortez asserted that the contrast between the two neighborhoods showed her the impact of economic inequality. "I grew up between two worlds, shuttling between the Bronx and Yorktown," she recalled. "It was that experience that allowed me to internalize at an early age that the zip code a child is born in determines much of their opportunity" (Griffith 2018).

After graduating from Yorktown High School in 2007, Ocasio-Cortez attended Boston University. During her college years, she worked as an intern in the Boston office of Senator Edward "Ted" Kennedy (D-MA). As the only Spanish speaker on staff, Ocasio-Cortez often fielded frantic calls from Latino residents whose friends or relatives had been detained by U.S. Immigration and Customs Enforcement (ICE). She claimed that this experience helped her understand the challenges undocumented people faced under federal immigration policies. In 2011, Ocasio-Cortez became the first member of her family to graduate from college, earning a joint degree in international relations and economics.

After completing her education, Ocasio-Cortez moved back to the Bronx and took a job as a bartender and waitress. She described her work in the food-service industry—in which undocumented immigrants perform an estimated one-third of all jobs nationwide—as a "galvanizing political experience" (Morris 2019) that increased her commitment to such progressive political priorities as workplace protections, universal health care, and immigration reform. In 2016, Ocasio-Cortez became a volunteer organizer for Senator Bernie Sanders (I-VT), who launched a progressive campaign seeking the Democratic Party's nomination for president of the United States. Although his bid ended in the primaries—and eventual Democratic nominee Hillary Clinton lost to Republican candidate Donald Trump in the general election—Sanders's campaign energized Ocasio-Cortez and many other young progressives.

In late 2016, Ocasio-Cortez received a call from Justice Democrats, a progressive political action group working to recruit working-class candidates to mount primary challenges against established, incumbent Democrats with centrist views. She was on her way home after participating in protests in the industrial city of Flint, Michigan, and on the Standing Rock Indian Reservation in North Dakota—two communities where low-income, minority residents were fighting against powerful corporate and government interests for access to clean drinking water. Inspired by her experiences, Ocasio-Cortez agreed to run for Congress. With the backing of Justice Democrats, she launched an insurgent campaign to unseat Joseph Crowley—a ten-term incumbent and one of the highest-ranking Democrats in the U.S. House of Representatives—in the June 2018 primary for New York's 14th Congressional District.

Although Ocasio-Cortez faced long odds of success, she ran an aggressive, grassroots, social media-driven campaign. She characterized Crowley as a career politician beholden to corporate donors and special interests who did not understand the everyday struggles of his constituents. "In a district that is 85 percent Democrat, overwhelmingly working class, and 70 percent people of color, we deserve a working-class champion," she said (Gray 2018). Ocasio-Cortez's platform included many of the planks that had resonated with voters during Sanders's campaign, such as expanding the federal Medicare program to provide health coverage to all Americans, establishing a federal jobs guarantee with a

$15 minimum wage, and increasing access to higher education through tuition-free public college.

As a Latina seeking to represent one of the most diverse districts in the nation, Ocasio-Cortez also advocated "immigration justice" throughout her election campaign. She called for legislation providing permanent legal status for participants in the Deferred Action for Childhood Arrivals (DACA) program and establishing a clear path to citizenship for undocumented immigrants residing in the United States. Ocasio-Cortez also expressed support for the movement to abolish ICE, which she described as a rogue agency that viewed immigrants and people of color with suspicion, treated them as potential threats to national security, and violated their constitutional and human rights. She objected to the Trump administration's escalation of ICE raids on communities and industries with large immigrant populations, characterizing most undocumented people as productive, law-abiding people who lived, worked, and raised families in the United States for many years. "As overseen by the Trump administration, ICE operates with virtually no accountability, ripping apart families and holding our friends and neighbors indefinitely in inhumane detention centers scattered across the United States," she stated on her campaign website (Ocasio-Cortez 2018).

In what many political analysts described as a shocking upset, Ocasio-Cortez garnered 57 percent of the vote to defeat Crowley by 15 percentage points in the Democratic primary. Her victory appeared even more unlikely given that she rejected campaign donations from corporations and political action committees, which meant her opponent outspent her by a 10–1 margin. "No single factor led to Mr. Crowley's defeat," Shane Goldmacher wrote in the *New York Times*. "It was demographics and generational change, insider versus outsider, traditional tactics versus modern-age digital organizing. It was the cumulative weight of them all" (Goldmacher 2018).

Ocasio-Cortez's primary win garnered a barrage of media attention and made her an instant political star. She coasted to victory in the November general election to become—at age 29—the youngest woman ever elected to Congress. She joined a "blue wave" that saw a record 102 women elected to the House, including 40 women of color, and shifted control of the chamber to the Democratic Party. By the time she took the oath of office in January 2019, Ocasio-Cortez had a larger audience on social media than the 60 other newly elected House Democrats combined, and her growing name recognition and political influence had netted her a coveted three-letter Twitter handle, @AOC. As she emerged as a spokesperson for the liberal left wing of the Democratic Party, however, she also became a target of scorn and derision among many conservative and right-wing commentators, who found her youth, inexperience, outspokenness, and socialist ideas alarming. Critics portrayed her as a dangerous radical and attacked her background, appearance, behavior, and intelligence as well as her policy proposals.

Immigration quickly emerged as a major issue for Ocasio-Cortez and other members of the 116th Congress, who took office in the midst of a federal government shutdown that grew out of a disagreement with President Trump over immigration policy. Trump demanded $5.7 billion to construct a wall along the 1,900-mile southern border of the United States, arguing that a physical barrier was needed to prevent immigrants from Mexico and Central America from entering the country illegally. He claimed that "migrant caravans" overwhelmed border security and brought drugs, weapons, crime, and gang violence with them to the United States. Democrats in Congress denied funding for the wall, calling it impractical and unnecessary, and characterized the migrants as families seeking asylum in the United States after fleeing political instability, persecution, and violence in their countries of origin. The standoff finally ended on January 25, when Trump signed a spending bill to reopen the government that did not allocate money for his border wall.

Ocasio-Cortez opposed border-wall funding as well as Trump administration policies that involved detaining asylum seekers at the border. A few days before her primary election, Ocasio-Cortez joined a protest in Texas against Trump's "zero tolerance" policy, which resulted in migrant families being separated at the border and children being detained apart from their parents. In July 2019, the congresswoman joined a group of Democratic lawmakers on a tour of immigrant-detention facilities in Texas. Several members of the group reported that detainees—including unaccompanied minors—were being held in deplorable conditions. Ocasio-Cortez said detainees told her they had not been allowed to shower for more than two weeks, had been forced to drink out of toilets, and had been subjected to psychological abuse by guards.

Trump and other administration officials denied that migrants were being held in cruel or inhumane conditions. The president also responded to reports of poor treatment by pointing out that migrants chose to break the law by entering the United States illegally. Conservative media outlets also claimed that Ocasio-Cortez had "screamed at" and threatened guards at the detention facilities and refused to follow the designated tour schedule. Critics also objected to the congresswoman's use of the term "concentration camps" to describe the migrant detention facilities, asserting that it unfairly equated Trump's immigration policies with the

Nazi genocide that resulted in the extermination of 6 million Jews during the Holocaust.

Ocasio-Cortez's vocal opposition to Trump's immigration policies made her a target of hostile tweets by the president. In one controversial message, Trump suggested that Ocasio-Cortez and three other progressive congresswomen of color—Ilhan Omar (D-MN), Ayanna Pressley (D-MA), and Rashida Tlaib (D-MI)—should "go back" to "the totally broken and crime infested places from which they came" (McNulty 2019). All of the legislators were born in the United States except Omar, who arrived in childhood as a refugee from Somalia, and all four are U.S. citizens. Trump's statement received widespread condemnation, with critics describing his castigation of people of color as foreign or "other" as a racist trope. Although Trump insisted that "I don't have a racist bone in my body," he continued to attack Ocasio-Cortez and her colleagues by questioning their patriotism and saying that they should leave the United States. "We don't leave the things that we love," Ocasio-Cortez responded, "and when we love this country, what that means is that we propose the solutions to fix it" (McNulty 2019).

Further Reading

Goldmacher, Shane. 2018. "An Upset in the Making: Why Joe Crowley Never Saw Defeat Coming." *New York Times*, June 27, 2018. https://www.nytimes .com/2018/06/27/nyregion/ocasio-cortez-crowley-primary-upset.html.

Gray, Briahna. 2018. "Two Very Different Democrats, Joe Crowley and Alexandria Ocasio-Cortez, Squared Off in Debate Friday Night." The Intercept, June 16, 2018. https://theintercept.com/2018/06/16/two-very-different -democrats-joe-crowley-and-alexandria-ocasio-cortez-squared-off-in -debate-friday-night/.

Griffith, Keith. 2018. "I Grew Up Between Two Worlds." *Daily Mail*, July 2, 2018. https://www.dailymail.co.uk/news/article-5908173/Bronx-candidate -Alexandria-Ocasio-Cortez-blasts-questions-working-class-roots.html.

Hillstrom, Laurie Collier. 2020. *Alexandria Ocasio-Cortez: A Biography*. Santa Barbara, CA: ABC-CLIO.

McNulty, Matt. 2019. "Meet 'The Squad': The Four Democratic Congresswomen of Color Trump Blasted in Racist Tweets." *People*, July 17, 2019. https:// people.com/politics/meet-aoc-the-squad-ilhan-omar-rashida-tlaib -ayanna-pressley/.

Morris, Alex. 2019. "Alexandria Ocasio-Cortez Wants the Country to Think Big." *Rolling Stone*, February 27, 2019. https://www.rollingstone.com /politics/politics-features/alexandria-ocasio-cortez-congress-interview -797214/.

Ocasio-Cortez, Alexandria. 2018. "Alexandria Ocasio-Cortez's Platform." Ocasio 2018. https://ocasio2018.com/issues.

Paiella, Gabriella. 2018. "The 28-Year-Old at the Center of One of This Year's Most Exciting Primaries." *New York*, June 25, 2018. https://www.thecut .com/2018/06/alexandria-ocasio-cortez-interview.html.

Dolly Lucio Sevier (1986?–)

Pediatrician who reported on conditions at migrant child detention facilities

Dolly Lucio Sevier was born around 1986 in Brownsville, a predominantly Hispanic city on the Gulf Coast of Texas that sits adjacent to the Mexican border. As a girl, she made frequent trips across the international bridge over the Rio Grande to visit relatives and attend family events in Matamoros, Mexico. Although Brownsville faced significant socioeconomic challenges, such as high poverty and low educational attainment, Sevier described it as "the greatest place on Earth while I was growing up" (Brownsville Kiddie Health Center n.d.).

Sevier attended Hanna High School in Brownsville, graduating fourth in her class in 2004. She went on to earn a bachelor's degree from the University of Texas in Austin in 2007 and then to complete medical school at the University of Texas Southwestern Medical Center in Dallas in 2011. While serving her residency in pediatrics, she married Graham Sevier. In 2014, the couple had a daughter, Clara.

Going away to college and medical school gave Sevier a new perspective on her hometown and its challenges. "Just as a shadow is only defined by the light that surrounds it, it was my departure from home that defines who I am today," she explained. "Looking back, I realize growing up 'under-served' was as if my experience and knowledge of this world was two-dimensional, and moving away literally added an entire new dimension. This realization only made me want to return and serve and serve and serve" (Brownsville Kiddie Health Center n.d.).

Returning to Brownsville as a pediatrician, Sevier recognized that limited access to quality health care contributed to the prevalence of chronic conditions among the city's residents, including obesity and diabetes. She decided to open a medical practice in Brownsville to promote the health and welfare of children from low-income families. Sevier viewed her role as "being the voice for the kid, the advocate" in an environment where families often lacked the resources to provide adequate attention and care (Raff 2019).

When Republican Donald Trump took office as the 45th president of the United States in 2017, his tough stance on immigration affected the atmosphere in Brownsville and other border towns. The Trump administration placed a strong emphasis on securing the nation's southern border and preventing migrants from Mexico and Central America from entering the country illegally. Trump promised to build a wall along the 1,900-mile Mexican border, for instance, and to step up raids and deportations by the Immigration and Customs Enforcement (ICE) agency. To some residents of Brownsville, Trump's rhetoric seemed designed to incite fear and hatred toward people of Hispanic ethnicity, such as when he characterized undocumented workers from Mexico as rapists and drug dealers, and when he portrayed Central American asylum seekers as "an invasion of our country" (Wehner 2019).

In the spring of 2018, the Trump administration enacted a "zero tolerance" policy in response to reports indicating an increase in the number of migrants—especially families and unaccompanied minors—crossing the border illegally. This policy required U.S. Customs and Border Protection (CBP) officials to arrest and prosecute anyone caught crossing the border illegally, including migrants who claimed to be seeking asylum from a credible fear of persecution and violence in their home countries. Supporters argued that the new policy closed a loophole that had previously allowed such individuals to remain in the United States until their asylum applications could be processed.

Since U.S. law prohibits minor children from being held in criminal detention facilities meant for adults, however, the zero tolerance policy effectively required immigration officials to separate families that crossed the border together. By mid-June, more than 2,000 migrant children had been separated from the adults who had brought them into the United States illegally. Many of these children were held in CBP detention and processing facilities near the border before being transferred to shelters operated by the Office of Refugee Resettlement or placed in foster care. Reports soon emerged of minors in CBP custody being kept in overcrowded and unsanitary conditions without access to basic necessities.

The legal standards for U.S. government treatment of unaccompanied migrant children in custody were established by a 1997 agreement that settled a California court case, *Flores v. Reno*. The terms of the Flores Settlement Agreement (FSA) required federal authorities to place children in "the least restrictive setting appropriate to the child's age and special needs." The FSA also required the government to house minors in "safe and sanitary" facilities and provide them with food, water, and access to medical care. Finally, the FSA mandated "prompt and continuous" efforts to reunite children with family members within 72 hours and limited the amount of time minors could be kept in detention to 20 days (Gruwell 2018).

As its effects became clear, the Trump administration's zero tolerance policy came under intense criticism. Critics derided the separation of migrant families as cruel, inhumane, and a violation of basic human rights. In the face of public outrage, Trump signed an executive order rescinding the zero tolerance policy on June 20, 2018. The controversy continued over the next few months, however, as various federal agencies struggled to reunite migrant children with their families. In addition, immigration officials continued to detain unaccompanied minors who entered the United States, including those seeking asylum or attempting to reunite with parents or other relatives who arrived earlier. Immigration attorneys argued that the circumstances and duration of many of these detentions violated the FSA.

In July 2019, a group of immigration attorneys invited Sevier to accompany them to McAllen, Texas, to visit the largest CBP facility in the country. Responding to reports of a flu outbreak that sent several migrant infants to intensive care, the lawyers asked her to conduct physical examinations and provide a medical opinion about whether immigration officials were ensuring the health and welfare of detainees as required under the FSA. On the day Sevier arrived, the McAllen facility held more than 1,000 migrant children. CBP agents refused to let her enter the holding areas where the children slept and ate, so she set up a makeshift examining room in an outer office lined with computer monitors. Sevier selected children's names from a list, starting with the youngest ones, and requested to see them. She examined a total of 38 children and then prepared a report outlining her observations.

In her report, Sevier compared the conditions the migrant children endured in McAllen to "torture facilities." She said the young children she examined described "extreme cold temperatures, lights on 24 hours a day, no adequate access to medical care, basic sanitation, water, or adequate food" (ABC News 2019). Some of the children exhibited symptoms of dehydration, malnutrition, sleep deprivation, and psychological trauma. More than two-thirds of those she examined suffered from respiratory illnesses. Sevier attributed their poor health to a lack of basic hygiene, noting that many children reported not being allowed to wash their hands, brush their teeth, or bathe during the weeks they had been held in CBP custody. She rejected the claim that the children had been sick when they arrived in the United States and instead blamed the detention conditions, which she described as "tantamount to intentionally causing the spread of disease" (ABC News 2019).

Sevier related the stories of several young detainees in her report. For instance, she examined one infant whose teenage uncle had been forced to feed him from the same unwashed bottle for days on end. When the infant eventually developed a fever, guards at the McAllen facility rejected the teenager's request for medical attention. Sevier asserted that "to deny parents the ability to wash their infants' bottles is unconscionable and could be considered intentional mental and emotional abuse" (ABC News 2019). Sevier examined another infant who had developed diarrhea. The baby's 17-year-old mother claimed that guards had refused to provide clean clothes, so she had improvised by swaddling him in some plastic-lined hospital bed pads she had found.

The reports submitted by Sevier and the immigration attorneys received significant media attention and generated public outrage about the horrific conditions at child migrant detention facilities. Inspectors from the federal Department of Homeland Security encountered "dangerous overcrowding" and unsanitary conditions at other CBP facilities. CBP officials responded to the controversy by asserting that the agency's "short-term holding facilities were not designed to hold vulnerable populations," such as young children, and insisting that agency personnel aimed to "provide the best care possible to those in our custody" (Raff 2019).

Trump blamed Democrats in Congress for not approving humanitarian funding to help CBP and other immigration agencies deal with an influx of unaccompanied minors crossing the border. The president claimed that his administration was doing a "fantastic job under the circumstances" (ABC News 2019). At the same time, however, Trump administration lawyers argued in federal court that the treatment migrant children received in CBP detention facilities complied with the "safe and sanitary" provision of the FSA. Congress eventually passed a spending bill that authorized $4.6 billion to improve conditions at border detention facilities, although progressive Democrats argued that it did not do enough to protect unaccompanied minors.

Sevier viewed her role in exposing the conditions faced by migrant children at the McAllen detention facility as an extension of her commitment to provide medical care to underserved populations. As a mother, she also felt a responsibility to advocate for children who did not have adults to defend their interests. "I mean, imagine your own children there," she stated. "I can't imagine my child being there and not being broken" (ABC News 2019).

Further Reading

ABC News. 2019. "Doctor Compares Conditions for Children at Immigrant Holding Centers to 'Torture Facilities.'" *ABC Action News*, June 24, 2019.

https://www.abcactionnews.com/news/national/doctor-compares
-conditions-for-children-at-immigrant-holding-centers-to-torture
-facilities.

Brownsville Kiddie Health Center. n.d. "Dolly Lucio Sevier, MD." http://english
.brownsvillekiddiehealthcenter.com/dolly-lucio-sevier-md.

Gruwell, Abbie. 2018. "Unaccompanied Minors and the Flores Settlement Agreement: What to Know." National Council of State Legislatures, October 30,
2018. http://www.ncsl.org/blog/2018/10/30/unaccompanied-minors-and
-the-flores-settlement-agreement-what-to-know.aspx.

Raff, Jeremy. 2019. "What a Pediatrician Saw Inside a Border Patrol Warehouse."
Atlantic, July 3, 2019. https://www.theatlantic.com/politics/archive/2019
/07/border-patrols-oversight-sick-migrant-children/593224/.

Wehner, Peter. 2019. "Trump's Words Are Poison." *Atlantic*, August 6, 2019.
https://www.theatlantic.com/ideas/archive/2019/08/what-trump-has
-done/595585/.

Donald Trump (1946–)

President of the United States who initiated the migrant family separation policy

Donald John Trump was born on June 14, 1946, in the Queens borough of New York City. His father, Frederick Trump, was a wealthy real estate developer, and his mother, Mary Anne MacLeod Trump, was a homemaker. As the fourth of five children in his family, Trump enjoyed a privileged childhood in the Jamaica Estates neighborhood of Queens. He completed his early education at the private Kew-Forest School before attending boarding school at the New York Military Academy, where he played golf and football. After graduating in 1964, Trump spent two years at Fordham University before transferring to the Wharton School of Business at the University of Pennsylvania. Trump received several draft deferments to avoid military service during the Vietnam War, including student deferments during his college years and medical deferments that he claimed were due to bone spurs in his feet.

After earning a bachelor's degree in economics from Wharton in 1968, Trump went to work for his father's real estate development company, E. Trump and Son. Three years later, Trump became president of the company and renamed it the Trump Organization. Under his leadership, the company shifted its development emphasis from middle-class rental housing to luxury hotels, casinos, resorts, and golf courses. In 1980, Trump launched the construction of Trump Tower, a 58-story Manhattan skyscraper that served as the headquarters of his business empire as well as his personal residence. In 1985, he purchased Mar-a-Lago, a private, luxury estate in Palm Beach, Florida. Trump eventually expanded his business interests to include a variety of other ventures. He operated an airline, for instance, served as a promoter for professional boxing and wrestling matches, launched a real estate training program called Trump University, and produced the Miss Universe beauty pageant. In 1987, Trump published a best-selling book outlining his business philosophy, *The Art of the Deal.*

Trump also established himself as a television personality. Beginning in 2003, he spent 14 seasons as producer and host of *The Apprentice,* a reality competition show that originally aired on NBC. On each episode, teams of contestants completed business-related tasks as Trump and expert advisers looked on and evaluated their performance. Afterward, Trump selected one contestant to eliminate from the competition with the catchphrase, "You're fired!" The final contestant remaining at the end of the season-long competition won a $250,000 job in the Trump Organization. As Trump's celebrity grew, he also made cameo and guest appearances on many television series and radio programs.

Over the years, Trump occasionally discussed political ambitions that included serving as president of the United States. He formed an exploratory committee to consider running for president in 2000 as a Reform Party candidate, for instance, before becoming a member of the Democratic Party in 2001. Eight years later, following the election of Democrat Barack Obama as the 44th president, Trump switched his allegiance to the Republican Party. He emerged as an outspoken critic of the Obama administration's policies, as well as a prominent "birther" who promoted the false conspiracy theory that Obama was born in Africa and thus did not meet the constitutional citizenship requirements to be president. Trump's status among Republicans rose following his keynote addresses to party leaders at the Conservative Political Action Conference (CPAC) in 2011 and 2013.

In 2015, Trump launched a formal bid for the Republican nomination for president. As the least experienced among 17 candidates in the primaries, he did not get much respect from political analysts, but his brash personality and bold proposals received significant media attention. Trump also gathered populist support with his raucous campaign rallies and promise to "Make America Great Again." After capturing the Republican nomination, he faced off against Democratic nominee Hillary Clinton, the former secretary of state, U.S. senator, and First Lady, in the 2016 election. During his campaign, Trump vowed to build a wall along the 1,900-mile Mexican border to prevent immigrants from entering the country illegally. He also promised to repeal the Affordable Care Act and dismantle climate change regulations that Obama had put in place. Finally, Trump pledged to create a probusiness climate by lowering taxes, reducing regulations, and renegotiating unfair trade agreements.

Trump came under criticism throughout his presidential campaign for making false or misleading statements. When the mainstream press questioned his assertions, Trump claimed to be the victim of biased media coverage and "fake news." Critics also uncovered evidence suggesting that Trump engaged in shady business deals, exaggerated his wealth, and paid "hush money" to bury negative information. Shortly before the November election, Trump became embroiled in scandal over a leaked tape in which he made sexually explicit comments and appeared to suggest that his fame entitled him to grope women. Trump also made several remarks during his campaign that critics condemned as racist, such as when he characterized Mexican immigrants as criminals, drug dealers, and rapists.

Although Clinton held a commanding lead in polls leading up to the election and won the popular vote, Trump prevailed in the Electoral College and claimed the presidency. He thus became the first person to be elected president without previous government or military service. Most political analysts considered his victory a shocking upset. Surveys showed that he garnered strong support among conservative, rural white voters driven by racial resentment and economic insecurity. In addition, investigations by U.S. security agencies found evidence of Russian interference in the election aimed at helping Trump, particularly through fake social media posts intended to inflame partisan debate and foment public discord. A progressive resistance movement formed to oppose Trump's presidency, and followers organized several large-scale protests as he prepared to take office. Millions of people around the world participated in the Women's March, for instance, on the day following Trump's inauguration.

Trump's immigration policies provoked some of the most intense criticism and debate. Immediately after taking office, Trump signed Executive Order 13769, which established a "travel ban" that temporarily halted immigration and restricted travel to the United States by citizens of seven predominantly Muslim nations (Iran, Iraq, Libya, Somalia, Sudan, Syria, and Yemen). Administration officials claimed that the controversial measure was necessary to prevent potential terrorists from entering the country. Opponents charged that it unfairly discriminated against Muslims while doing nothing to reduce the threat of terrorism. In the fall of 2017, the Trump administration drastically reduced the annual cap on the number of refugees admitted into the United States. Critics contended that administration officials ignored, suppressed, or manipulated data suggesting that refugees had a positive impact on the nation's economy that far exceeded the cost of resettlement.

Many of Trump's proposed immigration restrictions targeted people from Central America and Mexico who entered the United States by crossing its southern border. Trump repeatedly warned about an "invasion" of migrants and demanded that Congress approve funding to build a wall between the United States and Mexico. An impasse over wall funding in the federal budget led to a partial government shutdown that lasted for five weeks. Trump also instructed the U.S. Immigration and Customs Enforcement Agency (ICE) to increase raids and deportations of undocumented immigrants living in the United States. He also threatened to rescind the Deferred Action for Childhood Arrivals (DACA) program—an Obama-era policy that enabled an estimated 800,000 people who had been brought to the United States illegally as children to work and go to school without fear of deportation. Critics pointed out that many DACA recipients, known as "Dreamers," had resided in the United States for decades and had no connection to their countries of origin. Finally, Trump proposed changing the rules regarding birthright citizenship, which were established under the Fourteenth Amendment to the Constitution, to eliminate the incentive for immigrants to have "anchor babies" to remain in the United States.

The Trump administration enacted one of its most controversial immigration measures in the spring of 2018 in response to statistics showing an increase in migrants—especially families and unaccompanied minors—entering the United States. The so-called zero tolerance policy required U.S. Customs and Border Protection (CBP) officials to arrest and prosecute anyone caught crossing the border illegally, including migrants who claimed to be seeking asylum from a credible fear of persecution and violence in their home countries. Administration officials argued that the new policy closed a loophole that had previously allowed such individuals to remain in the United States until their asylum applications could be processed.

Since U.S. law prohibits minor children from being held in criminal detention facilities meant for adults, the zero tolerance policy effectively required immigration officials to separate families that crossed the border together. By mid-June, more than 2,000 migrant children had been separated from the adults who had accompanied them across the border. Reports soon emerged of traumatized children being held in crowded and unsanitary conditions without adequate supervision or access to basic necessities. In addition, federal agencies failed to track the whereabouts of some children so they could be reunited with family members. In some instances, parents were deported without being able to locate or reclaim their children, who remained in the United States.

As its effects became clear, the Trump administration's zero tolerance policy came under intense criticism. Opponents derided the separation of families as inhumane and a violation of human rights. Some administration officials blamed adult migrants, arguing that they knowingly put their children in harm's way by entering the United States illegally. Trump falsely claimed that the Obama administration was responsible for the family separation policy and insisted that only Congress could end the crisis. "I hate the children being taken away," he said. "The Democrats have to change their law. That's their law" (McArdle 2018). In the face of public outrage, Trump signed an executive order rescinding the policy on June 20, 2018. The controversy continued over the next few months, however, as various federal agencies struggled to reunite migrant children with their families.

Even after Trump rescinded the family separation policy, immigration officials continued to detain unaccompanied minors who entered the United States, including those seeking asylum or attempting to reunite with parents or other relatives who arrived earlier. Immigration attorneys, doctors, progressive lawmakers, journalists, and other observers who visited CBP detention facilities reported that migrants—including children—were being held in deplorable conditions and lacked access to basic necessities. Trump blamed Democrats in Congress for not approving humanitarian funding to help CBP and other immigration agencies deal with an influx of unaccompanied minors crossing the border. The president claimed that his administration was doing a "fantastic job under the circumstances" (ABC News 2019).

In August 2019, Trump directed the Department of Justice to mount a legal challenge to the Flores Settlement Agreement (FSA), a 1997 consent decree that established standards for the U.S. government's treatment of unaccompanied migrant children in custody. The terms of the FSA required federal authorities to house minors in "safe and sanitary" facilities, provide them with food and other necessities, and release them from detention within 20 days. Trump administration officials described the FSA as an outdated measure that fueled the humanitarian crisis by providing incentives to bring children across the border. "The *Flores* loophole acts as a magnet, drawing more and more alien families to make the dangerous journey to our border," according to a White House fact sheet. "The *Flores* loophole essentially gives a free pass into the interior of the

United States to many aliens who arrive at the border with a minor" (White House 2019).

In his personal life, Trump has been married three times—to Czech model Ivana Zelníčková (1977–1992), actress Marla Maples (1993–1999), and Slovenian model Melania Knauss (2005–)—and has five children, Donald Jr., Ivanka, Eric, Tiffany, and Barron.

Further Reading

ABC News. 2019. "Doctor Compares Conditions for Children at Immigrant Holding Centers to 'Torture Facilities.'" ABC Action News, June 24, 2019. https://www.abcactionnews.com/news/national/doctor-compares -conditions-for-children-at-immigrant-holding-centers-to-torture -facilities.

Amadeo, Kimberly. 2019. "Donald Trump on Immigration." The Balance, August 13, 2019. https://www.thebalance.com/donald-trump-immigration-impact -on-economy-4151107.

"Donald Trump Fast Facts." CNN, February 12, 2020. https://www.cnn.com /2013/07/04/us/donald-trump-fast-facts/index.html.

McArdle, Mairead. 2018. "White House Blames Democrats for Separation of Families at Border." *National Review*, June 15, 2018. https://www.national review.com/news/white-house-blames-democrats-for-separation-of -families-at-border/.

White House. 2019. "President Donald J. Trump Is Taking Action to Close the Loopholes That Fuel the Humanitarian Crisis on Our Border." Fact Sheet, August 21, 2019. https://www.whitehouse.gov/briefings-statements/president -donald-j-trump-taking-action-close-loopholes-fuel-humanitarian-crisis -border/.

Further Resources

Immigration and the U.S.–Mexico Border

Cantú, Francisco. 2018. *The Line Becomes a River: Dispatches from the Border.* New York: Riverhead Books.

Chishti, Muzaffar, Doris Meissner, and Claire Bergeron. 2011. "At Its 25th Anniversary, IRCA's Legacy Lives On." Migration Policy Institute, November 16, 2011. https://www.migrationpolicy.org/article/its-25th-anniversary -ircas-legacy-lives.

Daniels, Roger. 2002. *Coming to America: A History of Immigration and Ethnicity in American Life.* 2nd ed. New York: Harper Perennial.

Daniels, Roger. 2004. *Guarding the Golden Door: American Immigration Policy and Immigrants since 1882.* New York: Hill and Wang.

DeParle, Jason. 2019. *A Good Provider Is One Who Leaves: One Family and Migration in the 21st Century.* New York: Viking.

Dungan, Ron. 2017. "A Moving Border, and the History of a Difficult Boundary." *USA Today,* 2017. https://www.usatoday.com/border-wall/story/us-mexico -border-history/510833001/.

Editorial Board. 2019. "All Presidents Are Deporters in Chief." *New York Times,* July 13, 2019. https://www.nytimes.com/2019/07/13/opinion/sunday /trump-deportations-immigration.html.

Gerber, David. 2011. *American Immigration: A Very Short Introduction.* New York: Oxford University Press.

Golshan, Tara. 2019. "The 2020 Democratic Immigration Debate, Explained." *Vox,* July 29, 2019. https://www.vox.com/2019/7/29/6741801/2020 -democrat-presidential-immigration-debate.

Gonzales, Roberto G. 2015. *Lives in Limbo: Undocumented and Coming of Age in America.* Berkeley: University of California Press.

Gonzalez-Barrera, Ana, and Phillip Connor. 2019. "Around the World, More Say Immigrants Are a Strength than a Burden." Pew Research Center, March 14, 2019. https://www.pewresearch.org/global/2019/03/14/around-the-world -more-say-immigrants-are-a-strength-than-a-burden/.

Gonzalez-Barrera, Ana, and Jens Manuel Krogstad. 2019. "What We Know about Illegal Immigration from Mexico." Pew Research Center, June 28, 2019. https://www.pewresearch.org/fact-tank/2019/06/28/what-we-know -about-illegal-immigration-from-mexico/.

Grandin, Greg. 2019. *The End of the Myth: From the Frontier to the Border Wall in the Mind of America*. New York: Metropolitan Books.

Hing, Bill Ong. 2019. *American Presidents, Deportations, and Human Rights Violations: From Carter to Trump*. New York and Cambridge: Cambridge University Press.

Kamarck, Elaine, and Christine Stenglein. 2019. "Can Immigration Reform Happen? A Look Back." *Brookings*, February 11, 2019. https://www.brookings .edu/blog/fixgov/2019/02/11/can-immigration-reform-happen-a -look-back/.

Krogstad, Jens Manuel, Jeffrey S. Passel, and D'Vera Cohn. 2019. "5 Facts about Illegal Immigration in the U.S." Pew Research Center, June 12, 2019. https://www.pewresearch.org/fact-tank/2019/06/12/5-facts-about -illegal-immigration-in-the-u-s/.

Lopez, William D. 2019. *Separated: Family and Community the Aftermath of an Immigration Raid*. Baltimore: Johns Hopkins University Press.

Massey, Douglas S. 2015. "How a 1965 Immigration Reform Created Illegal Immigration." *Washington Post*, September 25, 2015. https://www .washingtonpost.com/posteverything/wp/2015/09/25/how-a-1965 -immigration-reform-created-illegal-immigration/.

Molina, Natalia. 2014. *How Race Is Made in America: Immigration, Citizenship, and the Historical Power of Racial Scripts*. Berkeley: University of California Press.

NPR. 2018. "The History of the Flores Settlement and Its Effects on Immigration." Capital Public Radio, June 22, 2018. http://www.capradio.org/news /npr/story?storyid=622678753.

O'Brien, Benjamin Gonzalez. 2018. *Handcuffs and Chain Link: Criminalizing the Undocumented in America*. Charlottesville: University of Virginia Press.

Pew Research Center. 2015. "Modern Immigration Wave Brings 59 Million to U.S., Driving Population Growth and Change Through 2065." September 28, 2015. https://www.pewresearch.org/hispanic/2015/09/28/modern -immigration-wave-brings-59-million-to-u-s-driving-population-growth -and-change-through-2065/.

Regan, Margaret. 2015. *Detained and Deported: Stories of Immigrant Families Under Fire*. Boston: Beacon Press.

Riley, Jason L. 2008. *Let Them In: The Case for Open Borders*. New York: Gotham.

Soerens, Matthew, and Jenny Yang. 2018. *Welcoming the Stranger: Justice, Compassion and Truth in the Immigration Debate*. Downers Grove, IL: IVP.

St. John, Rachel. 2011. *Line in the Sand: A History of the Western U.S.-Mexico Border*. New York: Oxford University Press.

Steinhauer, Jason, and Julia Young. 2015. "How Mexican Immigration to the U.S. Has Evolved." *Time*, March 12, 2015. https://time.com/3742067/history -mexican-immigration/.

Urrea, Luis Alberto. 2004. *The Devil's Highway: A True Story*. Boston: Little, Brown.

Zolberg, Aristide. 2006. *A Nation by Design: Immigration Policy in the Fashioning of America*. Boston: Harvard University Press.

President Donald Trump's Immigration Policy and Rhetoric

Amadeo, Kimberly. 2019. "Donald Trump on Immigration." The Balance, August 13, 2019. https://www.thebalance.com/donald-trump-immigration -impact-on-economy-4151107.

Cadelago, Christopher, and Ted Hesson. 2018. "Why Trump Is Talking Nonstop about the Migrant Caravan." *Politico*, October 23, 2018. https://www .politico.com/story/2018/10/23/trump-caravan-midterm-elections -875888.

Campbell, Monica. 2019. "Trump's Hard-Line Immigration Policies Build on the History of Former US Presidents." PRI's *The World*, July 12, 2019. https:// www.pri.org/stories/2019-07-12/trumps-hard-line-immigration-policies -build-history-former-us-presidents.

Davis, Julie Hirschfeld, and Michael D. Shear. 2019. *Border Wars: Inside Trump's Assault on Immigration*. New York: Simon and Schuster.

Elving, Ron. 2019. "With Latest Nativist Rhetoric, Trump Takes America Back to Where It Came From." NPR, July 16, 2019. https://www.npr.org/2019/07 /16/742000247/with-latest-nativist-rhetoric-trump-takes-america-back -to-where-it-came-from.

Fritze, John. 2019. "Trump Used Words Like 'Invasion' and 'Killer' to Discuss Immigrants at Rallies 500 Times: *USA TODAY* Analysis." *USA Today*, August 8, 2019. https://www.usatoday.com/story/news/politics/elections /2019/08/08/trump-immigrants-rhetoric-criticized-el-paso-dayton -shootings/1936742001/.

Gomez, Alan. 2018. "Tracking Trump's Many Threats, Claims on Immigration, Caravan Ahead of Midterm Elections." *USA Today*, November 1, 2018. https://www.usatoday.com/story/news/politics/elections/2016/2018/11 /01/donald-trump-immigration-migrant-caravan-central-america -asylum-midterm-elections/1846817002/.

Graham, David A. 2018. "Why Trump Can't Understand Immigration from 'Shithole Countries.'" *Atlantic*, January 11, 2018. https://www.theatlantic .com/politics/archive/2018/01/trump-haiti-el-salvador-africa/550358/.

Haslett, Cheyenne. 2019. "Fact Check: Trump's Claims on Undocumented Immigrant Crime Rates." *ABC News*, January 16, 2019. https://abcnews .go.com/Politics/fact-check-trumps-claims-illegal-immigrant-crime -rates/story?id=60311860.

Kullgren, Ian, Ted Hesson, and Anita Kumar. 2019. "Trump Weighs Plan to Choke Off Asylum for Central Americans." *Politico*, May 30, 2019. https:// www.politico.com/story/2019/05/30/asylum-restrictions-trump-central -america-1489012.

Kwong, Jessica. 2019. "Donald Trump Says 'Chain Migration' Immigrants 'Are Not the People That We Want'—That Includes Melania's Parents." *Newsweek*, January 14, 2019. https://www.newsweek.com/donald-trump-chain-migration-immigrants-melania-1291210.

Merkley, Jeff. 2019. *America Is Better Than This: Trump's War Against Migrant Families*. New York and Boston: Twelve Books.

Phillips, Amber. 2017. "'They're Rapists.' President Trump's Campaign Launch Speech Two Years Later, Annotated." *Washington Post*, June 16, 2017. https://www.washingtonpost.com/news/the-fix/wp/2017/06/16/theyre-rapists-presidents-trump-campaign-launch-speech-two-years-later-annotated/.

Pierce, Sarah, Jessica Bolter, and Andrew Selee. 2018a. "Trump's First Year on Immigration Policy: Rhetoric vs. Reality." Migration Policy Institute, January 2018. https://www.migrationpolicy.org/research/trump-first-year-immigration-policy-rhetoric-vs-reality.

Pierce, Sarah, Jessica Bolter, and Andrew Selee. 2018b. "U.S. Immigration Policy under Trump: Deep Changes and Lasting Impacts." Migration Policy Institute, July 2018. https://www.migrationpolicy.org/research/us-immigration-policy-trump-deep-changes-impacts.

Rucker, Philip. 2019. "'How Do You Stop These People?' Trump's Anti-Immigrant Rhetoric Looms over El Paso Massacre." *Washington Post*, August 4, 2019. https://www.washingtonpost.com/politics/how-do-you-stop-these-people-trumps-anti-immigrant-rhetoric-looms-over-el-paso-massacre/2019/08/04/62d0435a-b6ce-11e9-a091-6a96e67d9cce_story.html.

Sacchetti, Maria. 2019. "U.S. Asylum Process Is at the Center of Trump's Immigration Ire." *Washington Post*, April 9, 2019. https://www.washingtonpost.com/immigration/us-asylum-process-is-at-the-center-of-trumps-immigration-ire/2019/04/09/7f8259b8-5aec-11e9-842d-7d3ed7eb3957_story.html.

Scott, Eugene. 2018. "Before the Midterms, Trump Harped on the Migrant Caravan. Since Then, He Hasn't Brought It Up." *Washington Post*, November 8, 2018. https://www.washingtonpost.com/politics/2018/11/08/before-midterms-trump-harped-migrant-caravan-since-then-he-has-barely-mentioned-it/.

Srikantiah, Jayashri, and Shirin Sinnar. 2019. "White Nationalism as Immigration Policy." *Stanford Law Review*, March 2019. https://www.stanfordlawreview.org/online/white-nationalism-as-immigration-policy/.

Wagner, Alex. 2018. "Extinguishing the Beacon of America." *Atlantic*, June 15, 2018. https://www.theatlantic.com/ideas/archive/2018/06/extinguishing-the-beacon-of-america/562880/.

Wehner, Peter. 2019. "Trump's Words Are Poison." *Atlantic*, August 6, 2019. https://www.theatlantic.com/ideas/archive/2019/08/what-trump-has-done/595585/.

Family Separation and Migrant Child Detention

Acevedo, Nicole. 2019. "Why Are Migrant Children Dying in U.S. Custody?" NBC News, May 29, 2019. https://www.nbcnews.com/news/latino/why -are-migrant-children-dying-u-s-custody-n1010316.

Bala, Nila, and Arthur Rizer. 2019. "Trump's Family Separation Policy Never Really Ended. This Is Why." NBC News, July 1, 2019. https://www .nbcnews.com/think/opinion/trump-s-family-separation-policy-never -really-ended-why-ncna1025376.

Chatterjee, Rhitu. 2019. "Lengthy Detention of Migrant Children May Create Lasting Trauma, Say Researchers." NPR, August 23, 2019. https://www .npr.org/sections/health-shots/2019/08/23/753757475/lengthy-detention -of-migrant-children-may-create-lasting-trauma-say-researchers.

Chotiner, Isaac. 2019. "How the Stress of Separation and Detention Changes the Lives of Children." *New Yorker*, July 13, 2019. https://www.newyorker.com /news/q-and-a/how-the-stress-of-separation-and-detention-changes-the -lives-of-children.

Congressional Research Service. 2018a. *The "Flores Settlement" and Alien Families Apprehended at the U.S. Border: Frequently Asked Questions*. Washington, DC: CRS.

Congressional Research Service. 2018b. *The Trump Administration's "Zero Tolerance" Immigration Enforcement Policy*. Washington, DC: CRS.

Davis, Julie Hirschfeld, and Michael D. Shear. 2018. "How Trump Came to Enforce a Practice of Separating Migrant Families." *New York Times*, June 16, 2018. https://www.nytimes.com/2018/06/16/us/politics/family -separation-trump.html.

Dickinson, Tim. 2019. "Trump Administration Argues Migrant Children Don't Need Soap." *Rolling Stone*, June 20, 2019. https://www.rollingstone.com/politics /politics-news/safe-sanitary-no-soap-beds-court-migrants-trump-850744/.

Domonoske, Camila, and Richard Gonzalez. 2018. "What We Know: Family Separation and 'Zero Tolerance' at the Border." NPR, June 19, 2018. https://www.npr.org/2018/06/19/621065383/what-we-know-family -separation-and-zero-tolerance-at-the-border.

Fetters, Ashley. 2019. "The Moral Failure of Family Separation." *Atlantic*, January 13, 2019. https://www.theatlantic.com/politics/archive/2019/01/trumps -family-separation-policy-causes-national-outrage/579676/.

Gelernt, Lee. 2018. "The Battle to Stop Family Separation." *New York Review of Books*, December 19, 2018. https://www.nybooks.com/daily/2018/12/19 /the-battle-to-stop-family-separation/.

Gerstein, Josh, and Ted Hesson. 2018. "Federal Judge Orders Trump Administration to Reunite Migrant Families." *Politico*, June 26, 2018. https://www .politico.com/story/2018/06/26/judge-orders-trump-reunite-migrant -families-678809.

Goldberg, Michelle. 2019. "The Terrible Things Trump Is Doing in Our Name." *New York Times*, June 21, 2019. https://www.nytimes.com/2019/06/21 /opinion/family-separation-trump-migrants.html.

Gonzales, Richard. 2018. "Trump's Executive Order on Family Separation: What It Does and Doesn't Do." NPR, June 20, 2018. https://www.npr.org/2018 /06/20/622095441/trump-executive-order-on-family-separation-what-it -does-and-doesnt-do.

Graf, Alex. 2019. "UN Calls for End to Migrant Child Detention Worldwide." *Globe Post*, September 16, 2019. https://theglobepost.com/2019/09/16/un -child-migrant-detention/.

Gruwell, Abbie. 2018. "Unaccompanied Minors and the Flores Settlement Agreement: What to Know." National Council of State Legislatures, October 30, 2018. http://www.ncsl.org/blog/2018/10/30/unaccompanied-minors -and-the-flores-settlement-agreement-what-to-know.aspx.

Hasan, Syeda. 2019. "Report: Migrant Children Coming to the U.S. Were Traumatized after Family Separation." KERA News, September 12, 2019. https://www.keranews.org/post/report-migrant-children-coming-us -were-traumatized-after-family-separation.

Hayoun, Massoud. 2018. "The Trump Administration Is Reportedly Separating Hundreds of Immigrant Children from Their Parents." *Pacific Standard*, February 28, 2018. https://psmag.com/social-justice/the-trump-admin istration-is-reportedly-separating-hundreds-of-immigrant-children-from -their-parents.

Jarrett, Laura. 2018. "Federal Judge Orders Reunification of Parents and Children, End to Most Family Separations at Border." CNN, June 27, 2018. https://www.cnn.com/2018/06/26/politics/federal-court-order-family -separations/index.html.

Jordan, Miriam. 2019. "U.S. Must Provide Mental Health Services to Families Separated at Border." *New York Times*, November 6, 2019. https://www .nytimes.com/2019/11/06/us/migrants-mental-health-court.html.

Kriel, Lomi, and Dug Begley. 2019. "Trump Administration Still Separating Hundreds of Migrant Children at the Border through Often Questionable Claims of Danger." *Houston Chronicle*, June 22, 2019. https://www .houstonchronicle.com/news/houston-texas/houston/article/Trump -administration-still-separating-hundreds-of-14029494.php.

Lind, Dara. 2019. "The Horrifying Conditions Facing Kids in Border Detention, Explained." Vox, June 25, 2019. https://www.vox.com/policy-and-politics /2019/6/25/18715725/children-border-detention-kids-cages -immigration.

Long, Colleen, Martha Mendoza, and Garance Burke. 2019. "'I Can't Feel My Heart': Children Separated from Their Parents at the US-Mexico Border Showed Increased Signs of Post-Traumatic Stress, According to Watchdog Report." PBS *Frontline*, September 4, 2019. https://www.pbs.org /wgbh/frontline/article/children-separated-from-their-parents-at-us

-mexico-border-showed-increased-signs-of-post-traumatic-stress-us
-report-says/.

McArdle, Mairead. 2018. "White House Blames Democrats for Separation of Families at Border." *National Review*, June 15, 2018. https://www
.nationalreview.com/news/white-house-blames-democrats-for
-separation-of-families-at-border/.

McCarthy, Joe, and Jana Sepehr. 2018. "UN Accuses US of Human Rights Violations for Separating Migrant Families." Global Citizen, June 6, 2018.
https://www.globalcitizen.org/en/content/un-us-human-rights-abuses
-child-migrants/.

Naylor, Brian. 2019. "New Trump Policy Would Permit Indefinite Detention of Migrant Families, Children." NPR, August 21, 2019. https://www.npr.org
/2019/08/21/753062975/new-trump-policy-would-permit-indefinite
-detention-of-migrant-families-children.

Ní Aoláin, Fionnuala. 2018. "Global Response to President Trump's Family Separation via 'Zero Tolerance' Detention Policy." Just Security, June 30,
2018. https://www.justsecurity.org/58783/global-responses-president
-trumps-family-separation-zero-tolerance-detention-policy/.

Office of the Inspector General. 2019. "Management Alert: DHS Needs to Address Dangerous Overcrowding and Prolonged Detention of Children and Adults in the Rio Grande Valley." Department of Homeland Security,
July 2, 2019. https://www.oig.dhs.gov/sites/default/files/assets/2019-07
/OIG-19-51-Jul19_.pdf.

O'Toole, Molly. 2019. "Family Separations a Year Later: The Fallout—And the Separations—Continue." *Los Angeles Times*, April 19, 2019. https://www
.latimes.com/politics/la-na-pol-family-separation-trump-year-later
-20190412-story.html.

Prisco, Joanna. 2018. "World Political and Religious Leaders Condemn US Policy of Separating Migrant Kids." Global Citizen, June 19, 2018. https://www
.globalcitizen.org/en/content/us-migrant-families-policy-world-leaders
-condemn/.

Radnofsky, Louise, Natalie Andrews, and Farnaz Fassihi. 2018. "Trump Defends Family-Separation Policy." *Wall Street Journal*, June 18, 2018. https://www
.wsj.com/articles/trump-administration-defends-family-separation
-policy-1529341079.

Raff, Jeremy. 2018. "The Separation Was So Long: My Son Has Changed So Much." *Atlantic Monthly*, September 7, 2018. https://www.theatlantic.com
/politics/archive/2018/09/trump-family-separation-children-border
/569584/.

Raff, Jeremy. 2019. "What a Pediatrician Saw Inside a Border Patrol Warehouse." *Atlantic*, July 3, 2019. https://www.theatlantic.com/politics/archive/2019
/07/border-patrols-oversight-sick-migrant-children/593224/.

Rizzo, Salvador. 2018. "The Facts about Trump's Policy of Separating Families at the Border." *Washington Post*, June 19, 2018. https://www.washingtonpost

.com/news/fact-checker/wp/2018/06/19/the-facts-about-trumps-policy-of-separating-families-at-the-border/?utm_term=.491a13132a7b.

Sacchetti, Maria. 2019. "ACLU Says 1,500 More Migrant Children Were Taken from Parents by the Trump Administration." *Washington Post*, October 24, 2019. https://www.washingtonpost.com/immigration/aclu-says-1500-more-migrant-children-were-taken-from-parents-by-trump-administration/2019/10/24/d014f818-f6aa-11e9-a285-882a8e386a96_story.html.

Sergent, Jim, Elinor Aspegren, Elizabeth Lawrence, and Olivia Sanchez. 2019. "Chilling First-Hand Reports of Migrant Detention Centers Highlight Smell of 'Urine, Feces,' Overcrowded Conditions." *USA Today*, July 17, 2019. https://www.usatoday.com/in-depth/news/politics/elections/2019/07/16/migrant-detention-centers-described-2019-us-government-accounts/1694638001/.

Sherman, Christopher, Martha Mendoza, and Garance Burke. 2019. "U.S. Held a Record Number of Migrant Kids in Custody This Year." PBS, November 12, 2019. https://www.pbs.org/wgbh/frontline/article/u-s-held-record-69-thousand-migrant-children-in-custody-in-2019/.

Short, Kevin. 2019. "U.S. Government Confirms Migrant Children Experienced Severe Mental Health Issues Following 'Family Separation.'" Physicians for Human Rights, September 4, 2019. https://phr.org/news/u-s-government-confirms-migrant-children-experienced-severe-mental-health-issues-following-family-separation/.

Small, Julie. 2019. "Judge: Immigration Must Account for Thousands More Migrant Kids Split Up from Parents." NPR, March 19, 2019. https://www.npr.org/2019/03/09/701935587/judge-immigration-must-identify-thousands-more-migrant-kids-separated-from-paren.

Southern Poverty Law Center. 2019. "Family Separation Under the Trump Administration—A Timeline." SPLC, September 24, 2019. https://www.splcenter.org/news/2019/09/24/family-separation-under-trump-administration-timeline.

Stuart, Tessa. 2019. "Children Inside Texas Detention Centers Describe Squalid Conditions." *Rolling Stone*, June 27, 2019. https://www.rollingstone.com/politics/politics-news/texas-border-children-parent-separation-migrant-detention-centers-853055/.

Sussis, Matthew. 2019. "The History of the *Flores* Settlement." Center for Immigration Studies, February 11, 2019. https://cis.org/Report/History-Flores-Settlement.

Taddonio, Patrice. 2019. "Inside a Shelter Holding Detained Migrant Kids." PBS, November 12, 2019. https://www.pbs.org/wgbh/frontline/article/inside-a-shelter-holding-detained-migrant-kids/.

Wan, William. 2018. "What Separation from Parents Does to Children: 'The Effect Is Catastrophic.'" *Washington Post*, June 18, 2018. https://www.washingtonpost.com/national/health-science/what-separation-from-parents-does-to-children-the-effect-is-catastrophic/2018/06/18/c00c30ec-732c-11e8-805c-4b67019fcfe4_story.html.

Ward, Alex. 2018. "How the World Is Reacting to Trump's Family Separation Policy." Vox, June 20, 2018. https://www.vox.com/world/2018/6/20 /17483738/trump-family-separation-border-trudeau-may-reaction.

Wood, Laura. 2018. "Impact of Punitive Immigration Policies, Parent-Child Separation, and Child Detention on the Mental Health and Development of Children." *BMJ Paediatrics* 2(1): e000338, September 26, 2018. doi:10.1136/bmjpo-2018-000338.

Index

About the Author

Laurie Collier Hillstrom is a freelance writer and editor based in Brighton, Michigan. She is the author of more than forty books in the areas of American history, biography, and current events. Her published works include three previous volumes in the 21st-Century Turning Points series—*The #MeToo Movement, School Shootings and the Never Again Movement,* and *The Vaping Controversy*—as well as *Alexandria Ocasio-Cortez: A Biography* and *Defining Moments: The Constitution and the Bill of Rights.*